DATE DUE

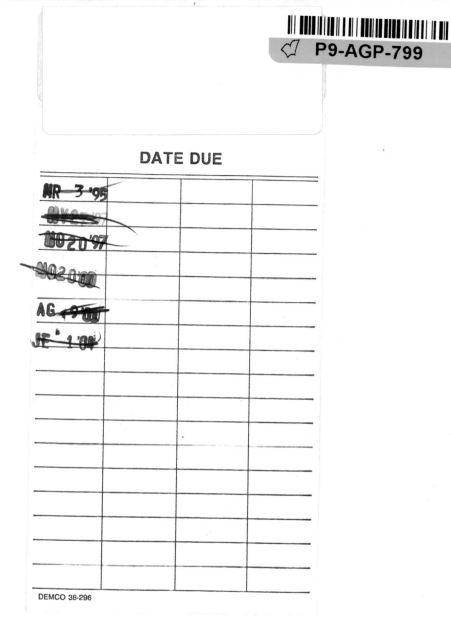

MR 3 '95

NO 20 '97

NO 20 '00

AG 9 '00

JE 1 '04

IN THE TRADITION

An Anthology of Young Black Writers

Edited by Kevin Powell and Ras Baraka

Published for **HARLEM RIVER PRESS** by:
WRITERS & READERS PUBLISHING, INC.
P.O. Box 461, Village Station
New York, N.Y. 10014

c/o Airlift Book Company
26 Eden Grove
London, N7 8EF
England

Cover design: Terrie Dunkelberger
Book design: Lisa M. Babb
Copyediting: Tracy A. Sherrod

ISBN 0-86316-315-7 Hardcover
ISBN 0-86316-316-5 Paperback

Manufactured in the United States of America

COPYRIGHT NOTICES

ACKNOWLEDGMENTS

The making of *IN THE TRADITION* has been an incredible four-year odyssey and would not have been possible without the support and dedication of many outstanding minds and souls: our agent Marie Dutton Brown, our publisher Glenn Thompson, Amiri and Amina Baraka, Sonia Sanchez, Jayne Cortez, Reverand Benjamin Chavis & The United Church of Christ, Lisa Williamson (Sister Souljah), the children of the African Youth Summer Survival Camp (1988), Mrs. Denise Cook, Rachel Denise Rustin, all the homies in Newark & Jersey City (guard your grill! Jersey's in there), Bob Law, the entire Hip-Hop Community (now that we know the ledge let's not fall over), The Dark Room Writers Collective of Boston, Black Nia Force (Big Up!), 100 Black Men of Rutgers University (Big Up!), Harry Allen, Nkuli Muhammad, Joette Harland-Watts, Stephanie Hughley & The National Black Arts Festival '92, Naadu Blankson, Cheryll Greene, Zaneta Williams, Sam Anderson, Lisa Teasley, MacArthur Joseph, Brian Gantt and James Gantt, Veronica Mixon, Tony Medina, dream hampton, Lorena Craighead, Trina Kisimi Smith, Askhari, Monifa Akinwole, Tamara Jeffries, Kimberly Ann Collins, Kimberly Knight, Veronica Chambers, Charlie Braxton, Trey Ellis, Elizabeth Alexander, Eugene Redmond, Jabari & Liana Asim, Ira B. Jones, Michelle T. Clinton, Jake-ann Jones (yeah, the heart of Harlem), Willie Perdomo, Paul Beatty, Miguel Algarin, Bob Holman, Christian Haye , and the whole posse from The Nuyorican Poets Cafe, Lamont Steptoe, Joseph Lewis, Scott-Poulson Bryant, Greg Tate, Joan Morgan, Danyel Smith, The African Poetry Theatre, A. Wanjiku H. Reynolds, Zayid Muhammad, Valerie Carey-Gosine, Rosie Rodriguez, Howard Nisbeth, Renaldo Imani Davidson (the hip-hop junkie artist is in da house no matter what!), Karen Carrillo, Kevin McGruder and "Home to Harlem", Herb Boyd, Don Rojas and *The Amsterdam News* Staff, Robert Allen, Jess Mowry, Asha Bandele, Tom Poole, George Sosa, Cyril Phipps (*Not Channel Zero* flips the script!), Tatia Davis, *Essence, Vibe, Emerge, New Word, The Source, Urban Profile,* Anthony DeCurtis & *Rolling Stone, Obsidian II* (one of the few Black literary journals that actually support young Black writers of various persuasions), Big Up! to editor Gerald Barrax, (All you other publications that's sleepin', toys ain't us!); and to any- and everyone who we neglected to mention, Thank U. Let's get it on!

And the editors offer a special word of thanks to Phyllis Lodge, who typed the entire manuscript; Lisa M. Babb, thank u 4 the fly layout, and Tracy A. Sherrod, thank you for the copyediting job.

Peace & Love 2 you all.

TABLE OF CONTENTS

◆FICTION◆

INTRODUCTION

IN THE TRADITION is a continuum of artistic, political, spiritual and psychological struggle. We are children of the post-integration (nightmare!), post-Civil Rights era, abandoned to find our way in a pot bent on melting our culture into mainstream oblivion (non-cipher!). We are the lost-found generation; the children of Malcolm and Martin and Fannie Lou and Ella. We are the Black Power cries of Stokely; the fire and blood of Watts and Newark and Detroit and now South Central; we are also the Black Panthers who stalked the steps of the California legislature. We were made in struggle. It is the fabric of our souls. Our voices are nothing new. Our hollers and screams will not go away. We are the echoes of the Harlem Renaissance–Zora Neale, Langston, Countee, Nella, Claude, et. al. We are the Black Arts Movement–Amiri, Sonia, Jayne, Haki, Askia, Audre, Mari, Henry, et. al. We are those poems and those stories. Like our ancestors, we got it goin' on and ain't goin' out like suckers.

We are the ART! We are the what is of what was. We are the next step after total silence, and, most importantly, we are the living. We are the movement, a new Black Consciousness Movement of poetry and fiction and art and music (yeah, hip-hop culture is our generation's contribution to the legacy of great Black music). We have been created; are the creators; are the creation. Our words are just the tip of the iceberg. Our art breathes. It is the life force which keeps us vibrating. It is the sirens, the whistles, the trumpets, the scratches, and the "yeah, you don't stop!" over the bass drum. Our words are reflective of the dawn, the rising of the suns, the next time fire Baldwin saw. We can't help ourselves. We must yell. We must write. It keeps us sane and our enemies in check. It is chanting for our people. This is for the people. Our people. Word.

Kevin Powell & Ras Baraka
July 1992

In the tradition of
all of us, in an unending everywhere at the same time
line
in motion forever

—Amiri Baraka

POETRY

*quite simply a
poem shd fill you
up with something/
cd make you swoon,
stop in yr tracks,
change your mind,
or make it up.
a poem shd happen
to you like cold
water or a kiss*

—Ntozake Shange

Viki Akiwumi is an award-winning poet and writer whose work has received wide acclaim. She has performed nationally and internationally. She has done readings of her work on radio and cable television programs. She is the co-producer of the award-winning poetry video showcase entitled "Nommo Vibes and Ancestral Melodies." Viki Akiwumi is currently working on her collections of poetry, a screenplay and a video on Afro-Brazillian culture. In the fall of 1992 she began her M.F.A. in creative writing at Brooklyn College. She dedicates her art to the power of the universe which moves through her life and work bringing constant miracles and blessings always. Ashe...Ashe!▲

➢ *different ones #6-Future Possibilities*
(An Aids Soliloquy)➢

it is a puzzle for the insane
this disease that has
carved itself like a slavers
lash into our minds.
we are walking timebombs
of sexual awareness
a sterile madness
afraid has become a synonym
for life
and our pockets are brimming with rubbers
for the moment when we fall into
the arms of lovers whose hands
are full of questions.
will we bend in this assault
will be feel tongues and lips
receding into white gloves
which take the place of moments
where we once breathed deeply
into each others mouths
trying to understand what
our mothers and fathers tried
to prepare us for
can we say that they have failed
as the reality of our lives comes
to dance under the gaze of truth
as we look at our brothers/lovers/
sisters/daughters open to eyes
that wonder and hands that offer
no assistance
as their bodies twitch in pain
rolling in spasms
wracking bodies already limping
from the respiratory disorders
of toxic racism in Harlem
and Chicago

mercury poisoning causing
the Zulu people to drop
like fallen warriors.
and meanwhile
we try to dodge
the bullets
aimed at communities
whose skin color caused them to
die
on this day
before they had their daily bread.
and we hit the dirt
like a jackhammer on concrete
we people of colors and sounds and smells
must raise our faces to look
at the dying
because their televisions
and radios
only spoke of hair relaxers
and skin lighteners
there were no public service announcements
to teach the young ones.
now we must rise
a collective union
with the hammers of our voices
and our hearts
we must break the glass windows
puncture the rubber gloves
so we can massage
the backs that yearn
for our touch.

2
when it was just beginning
rumours of a plague setting us up
for madness
moving us into delirium
international borders closing
master lists of people infected
men/women/children/babies being

led to prisons disguised as hospitals
led like the prisoners at Auschwitz
or the long lines of human flesh
walking onto the planks
at Goree Island.
it is possible for this madness
to come to reality
to flourish
like the skunk cabbage
under our feet
this disease in its beginning
we turned our eyes
whispered softly
and twisted our mouths
at this "gay disease"
we lived as we have always lived
and yet
when Uncle Henry and Auntie Rhonda
and Sister Maybelle from round the
corner
stopped going to the store
stopped going to the fish market
stopped going to pick up the mail
stopped going to get hair done
and nails fixed
we whispered but nobody really wondered
nobody really saw their bodies lying
covered with sores
coughing and wondering how to endure
pain that cripples.
let us lift our eyes
out of illusion
so that we may see
our brown faces
our red faces
our white faces
dying of this disease
killing so swiftly
so many

we must light the candles as
knowledge descends like lightening
we must light the candles
for the IV drug users
and pass them a needle they
can call their own.
we must light the candles for the gay
and bisexual man whose choice
of difference is not the problem now
the problem is when he is treated like a beast
made to lie down until bedsores
become gaping holes
bleeding.
light the candles for the babies
crying in their own urine
in a dark ward as people pass
with earplugs that keep out the
sound of their own pain
light the candles for the Latina woman
hiding in a small room under a blanket
of fear
machismo keeps her tears quiet like
the morning dew that settles in El Barrio
light the candles for the bodies being
lowered in the earth
our eyes must be clear
our hearts strong
as we seek to know this disease
as we realize
that our babies will soon become
museum pieces to gaze upon
when we wish to remember their smiles.
we must use the light
as we seek to understand the movements
of our arms
our legs
our eyes
we must know this disease
so that once again

we can reach out to
our lovers/mothers/fathers/babies
smiling
into a hologram of future possibilities▲

➤*Unconditionals #3*➤

touch me
in this place
before the rose
unwatered
dries
and
gives itself
to
the
wind▲

Elizabeth Alexander was born in New York City in 1962 and grew up in Washington, DC. She received her B.A. from Yale University, her M.A. from Boston University, and is currently completing her Ph.D. at the University of Pennsylvania. Her first book of poems, *The Venus Hottentot*, was issued as part of the Callaloo Poetry Series (University Press of Virginia, 1990). Her poems and fiction have appeared in numerous publications, including *Black American Literature Forum*, *The American Voice*, *American Poetry Review* and *The Southern Review*. She reviews contemporary literature for *The Village Voice* and other periodicals. Currently she is assistant professor of English at the University of Chicago. She is a 1992 recipient of the NEA artist grant.▲

➤ *Nineteen* ➤

That summer in Culpeper, all there was to eat was white:
cauliflower, flounder, white sauce, white ice-cream.
I snuck around with an older man who didn't tell me
he was married. I was the baby, drinking rum and Coke
while the men smoked reefer they'd stolen from the campers.
I tiptoed with my lover to poison-ivied fields, camp vans.
I never slept. Each fortnight I returned to the city,
black and dusty, with a garbage bag of dirty clothes.

At nineteen it was my first summer away from home.
His beard smelled musty. His eyes were black. "The ladies love
                                        my hair,"
he'd say, and like a fool I'd smile. He knew everything
about marijuana, how dry it had to be to burn,
how to crush it, sniff it, how to pick the seeds out. He said
he learned it all in Vietnam. He brought his sons to visit
after one of his days off. I never imagined a mother.
"Can I steal a kiss?" he said, the first thick night in the
                                        field.
I asked and asked about Vietnam, how each scar felt,
what combat was like, how the jungle smelled. He listened
to a lot of Marvin Gaye, was all he said, and grabbed
between my legs. I'd creep to my cot before morning.
I'd eat that white food. This was before I understood
that nothing could be ruined in one stroke. A sudden
storm came hard one night; he bolted up inside the van.
"The rain sounded just like that," he said, "on the roofs there."▲

➤ *Today's News* ➤

Heavyweight champion of the world Mike Tyson
broke his fist in a street brawl in Harlem
at three a.m. outside an all-night clothing store
where he was buying an 800 dollar, white
leather coat. The other dude, on TV, said,
"It was a sucker punch." Mohammed Ali said
"Tyson ain't pretty enough to be a heavyweight
champion of the world." Years ago a new Ali
threw his Olympic gold into the Kentucky
River, said he'd get it when black people were truly
free in this country. In South Africa there is a dance
that says we are fed up we have no work you have
struck a rock. I saw it on today's news.

I didn't want to write a poem that said "blackness
is," because we know better than anyone
that we are not one or ten or ten thousand things.
Not one poem. We could count ourselves forever
and never agree on the number. When the first
black Olympic gymnast was black and on TV, I called
home to say it was colored on channel three
in nineteen eighty-eight. Most mornings these days
Ralph Edwards comes into the bedroom and says, "Elizabeth,
this is your life. Get up and look for color,
look for color everywhere." ▲

➤ *The Venus Hottentot* ➤
(1825)

I. Cuvier

Science, science, science!
Everything is beautiful

blown-up beneath my glass.
Colors dazzle insect wings.

A drop of water swirls
like marble. Ordinary

crumbs become stalactites
set in perfect angles

of geometry I'd thought
impossible. Few will

ever see what I see
through this microscope.

Cranial measurements
crowd my notebook pages,

and I am moving closer,
close to how these numbers

signify aspects of
national character.

Her genitalia
will float inside a labelled

pickling jar in the *Musée
de l'Homme* on a shelf

above Broca's brain:

"The Venus Hottentot."
Elegant facts await me.
Small things in this world are mine.

II.

There is unexpected sun today
in London, and the clouds that
most days sift into this cage
where I am working have dispersed.
I am a black cutout against
a captive blue sky, pivoting
nude so the paying audience
can view my naked buttocks.

I am called "Venus Hottentot."
I left Capetown with a promise
of revenue: half the profits
and my passage home: A boon!
Master's brother proposed the trip;
the magistrate granted me leave.
I would return to my family
a duchess, with watered silk

dresses and money to grow food,
rouge and powders in glass pots,
silver scissors, a lorgnette,
voile and tulle instead of flax,
cerulean blue instead
of indigo. My brother would
devour sugar-studded non-
pareils, pale taffy, damask plums.

That was years ago. London's
circuses are florid and filthy,
swarming with cabbage-smelling
citizens who stare and query,
"Is it muscle? bone? or fat?"
My neighbor to the left is

The Sapient Pig, "The Only
Scholar of His Race." He plays
at cards, tells time and fortunes
by scraping his hooves. Behind
me is Prince Kar-mi, who arches
like a rubber tree and stares back
at the crowd from under the crook
of his knee. A professional
animal trainer shouts my cues.
There are singing mice here.

"The Ball of Duchess DuBarry":
In the engraving I lurch
toward the bellesdames, mad-eyed, and
they swoon. Men in capes and pince-nez
shield them. Tassels dance at my hips.
In this newspaper lithograph
my buttocks are shown swollen
and luminous as a planet.

Monsieur Cuvier investigates
between my legs, poking, prodding,
sure of his hypothesis.
I half-expected him to pull silk
scarves from inside me, paper poppies,
then a rabbit! He complains
at my scent and does not think
I comprehend, but I speak

English. I speak Dutch. I speak
a little French as well, and
languages Monsieur Cuvier
will never know have names.
Now I am bitter and now
I am sick. I eat brown bread,
drink rancid broth. I miss good sun,
miss Mother's *sadza*. My stomach

is frequently queasy from mutton

chops, pale potatoes, blood sausage.
I was certain that this would be
better than farm life. I am
the family entrepreneur!
But there are hours in every day
to conjure my imaginary
daughters, in banana shirts

and ostrich-feather fans.
Since my own genitals are public
I have made other parts private.
In my silence I possess
mouth, larynx, brain, in a single
gesture, I rub my hair
with lanolin, and pose in profile
like a painted Nubian

archer, imagining gold leaf
woven through my hair, and diamonds.
Observe the wordless Odalisque.
I have not forgotten my Xhosa
clicks. My flexible tongue
and healthy mouth bewilder
this man with his rotting teeth.
If he were to let me rise up

from this table, I'd spirit
his knives and cut out his black heart,
seal it with science fluid inside
a Bell jar, place it on a low
shelf in a white man's museum
so the whole world could see
it was shriveled and hard,
geometric, deformed, unnatural.▲

Sibby Anderson-Thompkins, 26, was born in Greenville NC. Having completed both her B.A. and M.A. in speech communication at the University of North Carolina at Chapel Hill, she currently serves as the assistant dean of students there.

When asked why she enjoys writing about the life experiences of African-Americans, Ms. Anderson-Thompkins states, "The act of writing allows me to find meaning and significance in everyday human experience."

She is in the process of compiling her first volume of poetry. ▲

➤ *To Love A Stranger* ➤

(for my sister-in-law nicole)

*Friday May 12, Nicole Broome Anderson
age 26, was found dead by her husband.
There appears to be no signs of any
foul play though...*

                                                it was exhausting

just back
from a weekend at the amusement park
cotton candy, chili dogs and the monster rollercoaster had left
unbearable pain
meanwhile
the light on the answering machine
was
blinking nonstop flashing
like a warning
but
the throbbing pain/disabling
ran down my back until
my husband/newspaper in hand/entered
unrecognizable
his face
             altered

                                 nicole was dead

suddenly
part of me was dislodged/uprooted
like fragments of a puzzle dismembered in one swift
move
i wanted/needed
to step back/pretend
it hadn't
happened/it was too
painful
that i would never seehertalktoherholdherGOD

i hate you

and i hate her for leaving

i look for her
in dark distant shadows
her spirit moving/filling
every part of me
you
my sister not my
sister
a stranger
who walked into my house
crept into my heart...▲

><i>interlude</i>>

i wuz goin' wif puddin'
at the time/he sure wuz sweet
on me
moma usta say
he hung around the house so much
you coulda taken him for a
coon dog sniffin' outa fox

one satday evenin'
jonny lee
come pullin' up to the house in this
big black buick
talkin' bout/woulda come go wif him to the cornerstore

well/
i ain't think nothin' of it/always wuz kinda
likin' jonny lee/so
i got my coat/chnged my tampon/so as
he couldn't catch no scent/and
wez wuz gone

wez wuz ridin' along/talkin'
and befo i noticed/wez sittin' out front
of the green meadow's trailor park
always wuz kinda partial to those big doublewides
wif two tone 'luminum sidin'/why
puddin' usta tell me some of the mo
modern ones come wif a waterbed
and a built in jacuzzi/anyway

jonny lee insisted that
we come on inside
said/we wouldn't be long/he
had some friends he wanted me to meet
i kept hemmin' and hawin' so/til finally
jonny lee said/he
wouldn't take no

for an answer
there wuz four of em'/includin'
jonny lee
they wuz sittin' around
actin' a fool/sniffin'
white stuff thru mini straws

jonny lee ain't say nothin'
he just got up/gathered the other fellas
in a corner of the room
                    COME HERE BABY
                WEZ GOT SOMETHIN'
                        FOR YA
but/
i sees his eyes/dark and strange/i know
somethin' ain't right/so
i says/nah now/jonny lee
i don't want nothin' you got
no/jonny lee/no

it/
wuz dark
the room filled wif unfamiliar
voices/smells/tastes
she
couldn't breathe/for the laughter
suffocated her
under the crushing weight
of their bodies
caused unheard pain
and
she lay there
motionless/on the aronhide
sofa
a river of blood
mixed with
sweat
and
semen▲

➤ brken promises ➤

...though the time seemed
most inappropriate
I eased forward
toward the tall
dark
stranger

        who stood in the corner

               of the room.

As I approached
I hesitated
frightened
by what I sensed
      as
uncertainty.

It is not
      easy
to relinquish the distance
it takes years
and experience
to acquire.
For after having been
brken
promises
shattered

             by the redundance of

meaningless love poems,
borrowed kisses,
and stolen
time,
I knew.

Yet,
in hope of something different
something better
something true

I continued
my pursuit.

Suddenly.
our eyes met,
I saw an endless pool of passion and desire.
And just before
the tall
dark
stranger
fell into my arms
THE TWO-TIMINGSHIFTLESSNEGRO TOTALLY DISSED
ME
AND WALKED OFF WITH SOME OTHER
WEAVEWEARINGHEIFER!▲

➤ *Epitaph for Willie*
Or Little Black Poet With No Future➤

today
i will b
a
poet
i
will writ of
beautiful blck people
ancient egypt
and fantastik aventures
in distant lands

p.s. for lack of refrence
i will have ta git
back
ta ya▲

Martha Anthony I call myself Martha Anthony, born on July 3, 1967 in the Bronx and raised in the Flatbush section of Brooklyn.

I graduated in 1989 from Columbia University with a degree in Spanish literature and culture with a minor in chemistry. I worked as a counselor in a women's facility in New York before enrolling at SUNY-Brooklyn School of Medicine, which I currently attend.▲

➤ Untitled #1 ➤

You cared whether I died or not
for you tried to kill me.
I came so close to death
but my inhibitions prevent me
from being so deliciously crass.
I cried internally, overwhelmed by you...
   and you never seemed to notice.
Never did I beg you to apologize for my demise
   for you did so instinctively.

"You're going to kill me,"
you whispered as I defouled your
   sword with my sacred blood.
Your fingers clutched at my back
as I mercilessly attacked you.
You, thanking me for the pain,
told me it was good.
And I took heed to your moans:
You wanted to die and I desperately
   wanted to be the one to kill u.▲

➤ *Untitled #2* ➤

So suddenly
in the distance shined a silver key.
If only we could reach it....
it shined a spark unknown.

And what's it for?
This rendezvous we witnessed means a whole lot more
   than just some entertainment
   or a onc-night stand.
And I still remember asking
this question
   about true love.

Well, I'll keep searching
   for forever.
I'll keep searching
   for true love.
I will forget him
   if I have to
and I will be the victor of my fate.

And "Yes," they say: "he is magnificent
   in every way."
But I would say that he's just phoney...
If only he could hear!

Yet with every tear that falls, I hear...
I hear his name. ▲

➤ *The Ugly Heart* ➤

I was the reflection of malevolence.
I saw my handwriting slant at an evil angle
   as I attempted to dispel my anger
   and pierce it through your heart.
I, being slighted, believed I was unpardonably violated.

Abruptly, without reason, the dam broke;
the water baptized my face
   and broke my heart as I watched my emotions
   and sanity fall at your feet.
I, being a proud woman, felt ashamed and defeated.

We can make an even trade.
I can abandon my weak spirit,
you can desert me,
you can hate me.

We can make an even trade.
We can nurture my weak spirit,
We can desert malevolence and the ugly heart;
We can hate strife.

And you can have my heart
You can have my soul,
You can have my emotions,
You can have my love,

And a kiss for every resolution. ▲

Sabah As-Sabah Poet, essayist and political activist, Sabah As-Sabah was born in 1966 amidst the camels and whirling sands of Harlem, U.S.A. Born and raised in Islam, Sabah tempers the anger inherent in his culture with the spiritual discipline inherent in his faith. Sabah presently works as a science and technology advisor. He is currently published in *American Letters and Commentary, Release, Poets and Writers Magazine, Nommo 2, Sing* and *The Road Before Us.*

"As a man, if my most worthwhile contribution to this new Black aesthetic is a scratch of my ever growing crotch and my backhand slid across the face of my Black woman, then I deserve to be an endangered species. The responsibility is in my hands." ▲

➤ *I'll Never Know No Sunday In This Weekday Room*➤

My voice drifts to the ceiling, like a stream of incense, filling
this sparse room with a thin layer of sandalwood.
Black sits I
Caressing a cold November
On old knees
and older dresses
Aretha sings
That man loves me like no other
swelling my belly with tumors
and raising up headaches behind my opened eyes
I want to take his foul seeds and crush them
chewing them into a fine powder to be swallowed and regurgitated
later into his four squat bifocal face.
My appeal rolls off of the junction that meets the ceiling to the
wall, gains speed, and knocks me on the side of my head.
His sting doesn't deserve to rest between the velvet blues
of my thighs or in the rapid roll of my folds
I'm on a mission
to twist and roll in insomnia's halls
where scented pillows are burned
and sweet songbirds in delicate flight are crushed
I stand on swollen feet
Ready
'Cause I got a scent on you
And what I'm smellin'
is as deadly as Hell.▲

➤ *Transition #2*➤

I'm a man
you pedestrian fool
One more glance
in my direction and I will strike
with a baptism so deadly
that one word from my lips will
thrust both you and your family
Back
to the swingin' vines of the caucasus mountains

I see you watching in
in between section A and C of the New York Times
watching
as the black and blue pencils roll over your lips and creeps
around the sides of your eyes
watching
as you manage to put the suit case, pocket book, portfolio,
shopwell bags, storage boxes, half-eatin sandwiches, paper back
books and the house plant you just purchased, between us,
as we ride the subway together

You want to remain safe
Do you actually think that a half-rotted azalea between us
is enough
to keep me from chewing up your very existence
to be spat out on this train today
creating a tension that no white man's water hose could break

Have I become predictable?
Am I now Malcolm Carmichael or Stokely X
They're all the same
Angry black niggah's on a mission to kill da' whitey

Well this is my boat and I'm the captain
A Pirate Jenny
who takes no prisoners
"cause there's nobody gonna sleep tonight"
"Nobody"
We ride today on sacred ground

Right under this track on 34th Street and 6th Avenue are buried
7 freedom fighters
who were thrown there in the 1930's
Every time I ride over that stop I get a feelin'
Somethin' happens to the brotha's and sistah's on the train
The relaxed hair stands up and locks
Proud and strong
The blue and green contacts pop out of the eyes
The track marks are filled and erased
The gold around our necks fall
causing a clatter that wakes us up
We have awaken on this movin' train speaking the mother tongue
rolling around the deep bad words in our mouths
But soon we are on 42nd Street and the spirits have stalled in
between stations
"We are experiencing mechanical difficulties, thank you for your
patience"
NO
I've been patient for 400 years
been goin' slow for 24
Pick de cotton
Go slow
Human rights
Go slow
A grandmother is shot dead by two racist police offers
Go slow
A white man rapes his black lover and then sews up her vagina
Go slow
A twelve year old boy is sodomized for not wanting to sell drugs
Go slow
And I can hear the Greek chorus singin' in one-eighth time
as I rape your wheelchair-bound father
"He was such a nice man, wouldn't hurt a fly"

I stir and feel movement between one and zero at the very bottom
of my soul

I smile

Prepare to enjoy the holocaust
"Next stop on this train 125th Street" ▲

➤*Jubilee*➤

I feel warm
in the muds of Louisiana
heating up my swollen ankles
as I make my way through the dead flies and agitated
grasshoppers
past deceased sojourners
who enrich my journey
with stories of rabbits and bears
I catch the wind in hair too heavy with history to move
and smell
the rank of honeysuckle and burning flesh
rolling underground,
I move to higher ground and run alongside the railroad
Feelin' the strength of my toes and the age of my oak
I take legendary leaps over plantations
"one step, two step, three step more"
Flying past the cotton fields and gliding over the corn fields
I call my childrens names
Come Harriet
Come Benjamin
Come Frederick
Come Alexander
I sing my song of Jubilee
sharing secrets with the sun
and shoutin' praises with the moon▲

Jabari Asim is a production editor at a large publishing house in St. Louis, MO. He is an assistant editor of *Drumvoices Review*, co-editor of *Young Tongues*, and editor of *Eyeball*, a journal featuring the best in poetry, cultural reviews and interviews. His work has appeared in *Black American Literature Forum*, *Obsidian II*, *Essence*, *Painted Bride Quarterly* and *Literarti Internazionale*.

Black bards bringing the message that we're needing
new word order and poetry is leading
unlocking lingo for the clue-less crowd
takin up the banner of the few and the proud . . .▲

➤ *Dumas* ➤

the eagle shall die
pierced &

plummeting
            twisting
                        turning
            blindly
                        burning

the dome shall fall
its high whiteness turned to dust
the final cleansing
                        we shall be avenged

and in that time our beating wings
shall be a Black shadow
upon the fading earth. the flight
of our soaring souls shall echo
the path of the sun across the
face of God.
                        we shall be beautiful▲

➤ *Harlem Haiku: A Scrapbook* ➤
(for Ira B. Jones)

1

morning brought strong rain;
the warm drops reached out to us
with welcoming hands.

we wandered between
Lenox and Liberation
looking for light in

Langston's lair, learning
the language of streets as fast
as New York voices

that spit swift words like
secret music much too rich
for our flat, slow tongues.

2

Harlem, Sweet Harlem
where Renaissance writers wrote
words that breathe Black fire.

3

Harlem, Sweet Harlem
where brave Marcus and Malcolm
faced down hungry Fate.

4

Harlem, Sweet Harlem
where noble ghosts watch and wait
for the rising time.

5

Harlem, Sweet Harlem
what deep secrets sleep beneath
your smoldering breast?

6

dusk brought long shadows;
the last light skipped and danced down
the darkening streets.

we stalked Harlem's haunts
like souls in search of something
to enchant our rhymes,

some kind of power
that makes the brownstones glow and
give off good magic
to make words dance and
solve the riddle of themselves
in perfect stanzas.

7

Sylvia's soul food
seduced our hearts and bellies
while we talked and dreamed.

recall the waitress
who charmed us with her beauty,
think of her smile as

I offer a toast
to hallowed, holy Harlem,
home away from home. ▲

➤*Hip Hop Bop*➤

well what's up, que pasa & a big hello
habari gani & a hi-dee-ho
share the glory of this story as I break inta rhyme
walkin the new way inside of time
stand back,
or choke on my smoke as I pick up steam
conjurin color, a zoot-suited dream
weavin word spells in a sonic stream
savin the thought nobody caught, puttin it down
beamin a scheme nobody dreamed, givin it sound

I'm a hipster lindy-hoppin in the corner of mind
twirlin toward the exit, strivin ta find
the light of true poetic expression,
breakin the back of systematic oppression
liberatin language, demandin attention
helpin hip hop to another dimension
jazz & rap in combustible conflation
crazyfresh lyrical prestidigitation

    Fee Fi Fo Fum
    clap your hands & give the poet some
    poundin percussion like Blakey & Max
       leapin like Lester when he's blowin his axe
    singing like a God, swingin like the devil
       juicin this jam to a higher level

rock it don't stop it, rock it don't stop
let me tell you the story of hip hop bop

hip hop boppin's beyond finger poppin
when the rhymes are rockin, there's just no stoppin
the full effect of blues-bombs droppin
& jazz words jumpin like drumsticks pumpin
'scuze me, while I git inta somethin

    spwee boppin dee bloop deedleoobleet

spwee boppin dee bloop deedleoobleet
unh! good God! somebody stop me,
I'd do it m'self but the spirit's got me
in a boogie bop trance
I'm a pinstriped dandy who lives ta dance
a jelly roll jitterbug
jookin the joint & cuttin the rug,
bustin rhymes fantastic
bluesy, bold, but never bombastic
always givin you my best though,
a manifesto
callin all souls: clap hands & sing
we can work wonders while our words take wing
leap slide spin like a dancer
sweep glide stimulate the stanza
re-defining form, rolling like a storm
cleansing like rain
nonstop hard bop in the manner of Trane

spectator shoes & porkpie head covers
gittin good vibes from my friends & my lover
struttin the 'hood in splendiferous vines
these are a few of my favorite lines

hah! I'm on the goodfoot, & my mike is smokin
poetry's the place where truth is spoken
my lyrics are limber & my tongue is nimble
splash me a dash of high hat cymbal

& listen for a minute while I break inta scat
jukin syllables & rhythm straight outta my hat
nonstop til I drop
when I blow that hip hop bop
when I blow that hip hop bop
when I
blow
yeah . . .▲

Askhari Askhari is...▲

➤ REcreation ➤

In the beginning God created the heavens and
the earth
Near the middle people of color took over to
show non-colored how it should be done

On the first day
we gladly destroyed all *their* missiles and
nuclear weapons
On the second day
we tearfully abolished apartheid from South
Africa, and established together and equal
On the third day
we lovingly returned America to the Native
Amerikans and put the reservations
back on reserve.
On the fourth day
we generously fed the Third World food, not
money
On the fifth day
we put the Ku Klux Klan and other white
supremicists on the reservations so our
progress would not disturb them.
On the sixth day
we *finally* went home.
We gave a housewarming party on the Nile River
and everybody was invited. We said let there
be darkness and
there was *only* darkness
and it was good
On the seventh day
we slept late cuz
we wuz tired.▲

➤ *Colorstruck* ➤

(4LW)

When you look at me
you see

a light skinned,
a yellow,
a redbone.

But when I look in the mirror,
Everywhere
I look
I see
the
gentle
explosion
of
Blackness▲

➤ ISALUTU ➤

This is for the men and women
who picked cotton from
can't see in the morning
until
can't see at night
or until polyester was created
and ain't get tired.
This is for the men
who slap high fives
when there ain't nothin' to be high on
and ain't got five cents
in their pockets to buy somethin'
to be high on.
This is for the women
who keep on keeping on.
And ain't got nothin' to keep.
To call their own.
This is for the peoples
who forgave what
they could not forget.
And NOBODY even said
sorry.▲

➤ *Circular Fate* ➤

white woman:

>Why did you sit there
>nonchalantly
>while *your* menfolk
>premeditated

our
murder?

And now, white woman:

>in desperation you reach out to me
>for strength.

How dare you call yourself my sister?

>*Fight alone*

I knew those

>*same navy blue eyes*
>would
>one day
>settle on you. ▲

"we who believe in freedom cannot rest..." sweet honey in the rock

asha bandele (Carol Bullard) was born-n-raised in new york city in 1966 / &
has been writing for about ten years / she has studied at various universities, most
recently hunter college / she is still seeking education, however / asha views poetry-
n-writing as one of several tools/to be employed in the struggle for freedom-n-
justice for afrikans / & thus views herself as a blackpoet not a "poet who happens
to be black" / asha is the former president of the audre lorde women's poetry centre
/ & the former president of hunter college's evening student government /
currently she is reading her poetry throughout the country with several other
blackpoets (ache) / while in new york, she continues to teach writing in state
prisons▲

➤*A Prayer For The Living*➤

(for kimson russell & the spirit of his family)

New York Times, 11/13/90: "...On Thursday, Kimson Russell was supposed to celebrate his 17th birthday...instead...Mr. Russell's family and friends will gather for his funeral..."

PART 1

a ringing phone & a hushed voice
breaks
the quiet of a sunday morning
   they shot veberly's son last nite
   he's dead
impossible, i think...
i must be in a nitemare
but the voice doesn't go away
& i am awake
awake & calling veb
offering words & thots
of support & sorrow
   words a mother ought never have to hear
(it is too frightening to ask the necessary question:
   will this be a/nother decade of dead children?)

so we plan this funeral
this memorial
this teach-in
this burial
worrying throughout there is no money to cover the cost

  a friend asks:
    but how is mother ever to have such money?
    how was she supposed to plan for this expense?

we'll have everything right here
veb says
in the community
she says

but its the trenches she means

for this is a war-zone
& we are casualties
each one of us
walking wounded
the scars seen
& unseen

PART 2

for kimson russell
taken at 16
for his mother & sister
his brother & grandmother
for the girl he loved
for the baby he made
for the father he never knew
nor
touched

for all blackpeople
who have buried their children/
as unprepared soldiers
in this war this war this war
we did not ask for
& cannot seem to escape
this war against black
this war against black humanity
raging on mean mean streets
called
sutter
&
euclid

for all those who have been taken before this day
for all those who will not be saved tomorrow
for all those whom no one remembers
nor whose spirits we honor

i submit this humble prayer

in the name of the mothers & the fathers
the sons & the daughters
the brothers & the sisters
the friends & the lovers

to those of us still living...
from this day forward:

may we walk forever in clarity
that we shall nevermore confuse
the enemy from the friend
nor be organized into gangs against each other
nor place material before soul
nor participate in our own murders

may we walk forever in honor
because within us lies the reality of who we have been
& the possibility of who we might be/come

may we walk forever in strength
for strength is the legacy
of the children of a people
who survived the middle passage

may we walk forever with pride
wherever we may travel
for our ancestors were founders
philosophers & builders
& they have willed us nothing less

may we walk finally & forever
in peace amongst our people
with respect & with dignity
despite our differences
for it is only us
as brethren & sistren
who can lead us thru these
the darkest of days...

ache

➤ 1980-1990:
A Poet's Personal Review➤

blasted
i was a 15/yr old junkie   waste
falling off the edge of
new worlds & each day
        who knew we would live past 21
glassy-eyed teenaged philosophers   we were
black & fearless
i hated ronald reagan living at home & me

moving in a small unarmed youthful army thru
central park
washington square
anyplace in new york where
you could dare to be
different
& stoned
        first priority:
yo!
who got the get high?
sinsemillia
cocaine
mescaline & mushrooms
        d.c. was a horrible city to live in when i moved there
        dry & dull
        bougie
        boppin to a planet rock beat
        the only herb you could find
        was soaked in embalming fluid
        nasty shit we smoked anyway
        & love came with desperation
        we both dug reggae & al jarreau
        but we screwed to sexual healing
        (everybody was doin it —
        trying to find fantasy in a marvin gaye song)
        i never did have an orgasm back then

or even learn how to fake it
but it felt good to be held & i took what i could
& stored it away like a prophecy
of what was to come

1980s
that decade fell on us like napalm
& we traded love & humanity
for porkbellies on the stock exchange floor
while policemen renewed their vows as klansmen
i was 16 & kids like hid themselves away
inside private journals & suicide pacts
cos they seemed like the only real things in an unreal time
when junk bonds could be worth millions
& human life worth nothing
& no one talked about africa
at least
not publicly
not even at howard university where i was a student
the girls in my dorm demanded
i stop playing my "witepeople's music"...they never heard of bob
marley, i guess &
i couldn't explain
instead i just got a walkman for christmas that year
& kept on trying

blurred
some years are blurred
ugly images flashing on a screen
i think they made another devil movie that year
whatever—reagan was re-elected
along with jesse helms who got 13% of the black vote proving:
        if you starve a man long enuf
        he's liable to eat anything
        including his pride

things moved so quickly
life was a sound-bite
negative campaigning

a 30-second spot
leaving no time to care for this dis-ease
after all it
was only killing faggots & junkies
& even blackamericans didn't make the connection
that it was killing sober/heterosexuals in africa too
til it was too late
& our own dead babies
began invading our dreams
as surely as they did
our nitemares

& while all this was going on
america murdered maurice bishop
& shit on grenada
lebanon
libya
the gaza strip
soweto
el salvador
nicaragua
panama
osage street (move...remember move?)
puerto rico
brooklyn
anywhere & everywhere there were people trying to make

while all this was going on
native americans remained captive in concentration camps
called reservations

in short

these were very sobering times
& even i had to abandon the drugs
since it was impossible for me
not to realize
being black necessitated being alert
being a woman doubled that necessity

TAWANA DID TELL THE TRUTH!!
& it was verified by a world fulla black women
whose fear kept us silent
but whose experience was mirrored in the eyes of that little girl's face
terror-stricken
sprawled like the venus hottentot
naked
for wite male perversion

the 1980s
yeah
it was
"the decade of excess" the media said
but they never did get past donald trump long enuf to tell the truth
excess of racism
excess of sexism
excess of dollarism
excess of wite privilege
excess of black poverty
vomiting the american dream on homeless streets
men
women
children   laid out
like yesterday's garbage
& we stepped over them like a crack in the sidewalk
or dogshit

still
very few of us were talking revolution

some students stormed their campuses crying
MONEY FOR SCHOOLS NOT FOR JAILS
which held more black boys than college classrooms did

wolfpacks
we were told
our children were animals
& they were cut down as such in that year
that horrible horrible year

when death came hard & fast at the hands of black children
who'd never been taught nuthin
but how to hate themselves & each other
from january to december
i lived in funeral homes
holding tiny caskets of babies
our babies
real babies
babies who'd had hopes & dreams & thots & names
they had names!
shinnique brown
veronica corales
shamel knight
pierre le rouche
laykama taylor
leviticus mitchell
alvin rivera
sharon shadou
john thomas jones
kimson russell
wilbur pollack &

this list is not complete this list is not complete

& even nelson mandela
public enemy
boogie down productions
african medallions
dreadlocks
kufes
& kente cloth
could not save these children
& a few of us began to wonder
if africa & revolution
hadn't be/come...saleable items
symbols
which could be bought & sold on any street corner   a fad
exchangeable for a job
(with pension)

keep the faith
we said once as high school seniors in 1982
keep the faith
we say today
but also, you gotta do the work, blackpeople, despite
difficulty
& circumstance
evil can't be done forever
america will pay for its crimes
what comes around really does go around
& we do
reap what we sow
if not for ourselves
then for future generations
eastern europe will eat itself up
in its new-found capitalism mis-labelled democracy
while ancient civilizations
the ones value-based in humanism
will rise again

do the work blackpeople
& africa will
prevail▲

Ras Baraka, 23, was born in Newark, NJ and graduated from Howard University in 1991. The son of internationally acclaimed writer Amiri Baraka and the poetess Amina Baraka, Ras is currently teaching in the Newark school system. An accomplished speaker, Ras has lectured and read his poetry throughout the nation and abroad and has appeared on several television and radio programs, including *the Donahue Show.* Active in Black/hip-hop communities, Ras is executive minister of Black Nia Force (the New York Chapter), a youth group, and has contributed articles to *The Source.* Ras is currently compiling his first volume of poetry, *Big Cities, Hometowns, and Ghettoes.* ▲

➤ *After-Word* ➤

Something strange happened yesterday
The sky swallowed the stars and everyone laughed
until their faces hurt.
Then death swept the earth
and there was total darkness
and everyone was sane
except the spotted creatures
who fled to the hills before the war!▲

➤ Five-O ➤

Darkness with white spots
or stars maybe!
hard, cold concrete
Pain from lead on the back of your head
Niggers in blue suits and honkeys in hats
Ropes have become primitive
and 9 millimeters are more effective
They've now dyed their suits,
traded in masks for badges,
And become equal opportunist.
Making it okay for everyone to beat Niggers!
Freeze muthafucker Up against the wall.
My father was killed in a war,
like Vietnam.
On a street, around the corner from My house!
got a new father now
adopted one, given to me by the state
loves to give orders and beats every muthafucker he sees!
get on the ground
up against the wall
hands up, behind your back
who got the drugs
where's your mother
Turn around
clear the corner
don't let me catch you around here again boy.
but I live up the street sir.
Move then Nigger!
You can't express your frustration the anger
as your hands clinch your hair
on top of your head.
As you peer down on a short white man
with a Napoleon complex
feeling your private parts
face red as his ass
contemplating being on his knees
like last night

But since he ain't, you payin' for it!
The gestapo lives in Harlem
I swear it. I seen 'em yesterday
After Hitler died they left Germany, moved to New York
said they wanted to be closer to McDonald's or Niggers
who eat McDonald's.
That way they can get rich and kick ass
simultaneously.
Freeze, up against the wall motherfucker
Cold steel resting on your cheek bone.
Caused by a rerun of a cowboy movie
starring Ronald Reagan.
Don't talk back they'll slap you in the mouth
Don't be intelligent
They'll beat you stupid
And don't run, they'll shoot you in the back!
Stand still and suffer
suffer
as your rights get read
with a gun to your head
They're just doin their job
protecting life, liberty and the pursuit of property!
and you were the property
Thus, you have no property
And they don't want you on their property!
So you trespassing!
And the penality for trespassing is death!▲

➤*For The Brothers Who Aint Here*➤

This is for the brothers–who aint here
For the strong brothers who are missing in action
For cool daddy pimp Long Legs who had seven children
three of them on crack
for my main man Big Willie Graham
who was shot by two white cops
before taking three of them with him   one of them was black
For Wausi Changa found strangled in his apartment
after coming home from a Black Nia F.O.R.C.E. meeting
For Larry Witherspoon–who went all the way through college
tried to marry some caucasian woman
too bad she was the boss' daughter
This poem is for the makers, the breakers, the no-stuff takers
the mixters, the tricksters, yeah and the cabbage lickers
This is for the brothers who aint here
Echoes of laughter
cloudy puffs of smoke
white washing wizards in the midst of darkness
You aint good for nothing black man
Death to you
Death to you black man
Dead black man
Black man dead
smells of death, movements of death, thinking of death,
dead thoughts living death,
death, death, death, death
This is for the brothers who aint here
You still the same man you were
When you first got here
Serving somebody else's cause
but only now you think you serving your own
And will kill anybody–who tells you otherwise–
if he's black that is.

For the brothers   you don't see
Before I go to bed at night
Burning tears like fire roll down my cheeks

As I think about all the brothers that could have made a difference.
But was too tough, too wild, too sane–to do so.
What happened to you black man?
where are you?
Where are those pyramid builders, those creators of sciences
and languages,
those starters of civilization, are you?
Where are you?
Where are you?
Where are you, black man?
This is for the brothers who aint here
I could scream until my voice disappears,
Think until my head bursts
Write until my fingers fall off
You evil sons of bitches
I want to squeeze you–until your very essence disappears
from thought
But, that will make me sane
And I'm insane–that's right
Crazy as hell, off my rocker, out of my mind

For the brothers who aint here
The community protectors, devil rejectors,
for the doers, and takers, the revolutionary makers–yeah.

For the brothers who aint around no more
I'm so sorry black man–so sorry
Sorry that we had to be oppressed
Sorry we didn't just wipe these devils out
Sorry for all the women we beat up–out of our hatred
Sorry for all the other brothers we killed out of ignorance
Sorry for being weak in times of courage
Sorry for being dead and taking you with me
Sorry for letting them destroy everything we had
Sorry for being everything opposite of what we were created to be
Sorry for all the dead drug dealers in fancy cars
Sorry for the lack of unity and run down communities
Sorry for not raising our children up to be warriors
Sorry for getting killed before I even became a teenager

Sorry for being born into slavery
Sorry for these sorry schools
Sorry, I'm so sorry black man, so sorry
Black man I'm so so so so sorry
I'm sorry black man
Sorry
Black man
Kill▲

➤ *I Remember Malcolm* ➤

I.
Ma Ma Ma Malcolm
Ma Ma Ma Malcolm
Ma Ma Malcolm
Ma Ma Ma MA MA Malcolm
even in your death
we are afraid
to say your whole name
or look to see
if the name we call you
FITS.
Ma Ma Ma Ma Malcolm
probably if
Spike
wuz alive when u were
he wd be clearer or
dead, huh maybe
at least that character wd be
definitely.

II.
Hey YO! Hey YO!
Hey Yo! Yo!
I knew a kid named him
named he
named Malcolm.
At least that's what
they called him.
He used to rob drug dealers
till he wuz gunned down by the police
on account that the only thing he really learned
how to do in school wuz steal.
yeah, I Knew Malcolm
he used to run with puerto ricans
cause he had red curly hair
he wuz known for pulling knives
and would cut you in a minute.

Who Malcolm, yeah
there wuz a guy named Malcolm
he went to school with me
they would always put him in slow classes
cause the teachers thought he talked too much.
yeah, I remember Malcolm
he wuz about seven feet and wuz dark black
he wore a two finger gold ring and an
African medallion
he would stand on street corners
and tell us how the white man wuz
responsible for
the shit we always found ourselves in.
yeah, I knew Malcolm
we were formally introduced in college
my professors would always say
his name in passing, or as quickly as possible
to get it off of their minds
to prevent any allergic reactions.
We always were assigned
to do papers on him
on our own time of course, but
the more I read
the more I wuz convinced that
I knew Malcolm
I seen him before
that he grew up with me,
and all the Malcolms I knew
in my life had one thing in common
they wuz determined to fight
by any means necessary!!!

        III.
Hey Malcolm
Malcolm
Hey you, hey Malcolm
Hey you
Hey he
Hey us

Hey we
Hey I
Hey Malcolm Malcolm
Wake up brotha
they trying to steal yr name
cage yr shadow
its them Malcolm
they
them
white boys
with blue eyes and green hair
smoking weed in washington square park
and niggers in short leather jackets
and rhinestone X-hats
needgrow executives
working for exxon
with kente scarfs
alligator shoes and
sweat socks with red white and blue
X's all over them
celebrating yr legacy
Hey Malcolm, Malcolm
check out the socialist white boys
with their papers at our meetings
controlling yr words
cldnt be found when you were alive
now that you are gone
they have become head whitey
the father of our ideas
like the same liars they claim not to be
Hey Malcolm, Malcolm
the village people want you malcolm
Macho Macho Man
They want to kidnap you from Harlem and
move you downtown!!
Mass produce X-hats, X-coats, X-medallions,
X-ties, X-shirts, X-lingere
and X-revolutionaries
Yeah Malcolm, they want you

your name, your footprints, your shadow,
they want to capture yr fire
make movies about it
bottle it
sell it
smoke it
get high off it
yeah Ma Ma Ma Malcolm
Ma Ma Ma Malcolm
Hey Malcolm Hey Malcolm
Hey Hey Malcolm
WAKE UP!!!!!!!!!!!

IV.

I should've wrote
this poem a long long
time ago
I would've saved some lives
then
Amerikkka is the place
that swallowed
Malcolm
where they killed our
brotha
while most of us watched!
Our screams weren't loud enough
to save his life
Our anger wuz not fiery enough to
have kept him alive
They killed our brotha
our enemies did
They murdered our
brotha
shot him down in cold blood
They killed him
tore his body apart
and he bled, he bled
all over our community he bled
Our enemies

they did it
stole the life from his body
they killed him
MURDERERS!!!!
in cold blood
while all of us watched(?)...
HEY MALCOLM!!
MALCOLM!
some things have changed
since you've been gone
brotha
but most things have stayed the
same.▲

➤ In The Tradition Too➤

(For Amiri and Amina Baraka)

[Death to South Africa long live Azania....!]

And they always aske me "who do you
aspire to be like?"
And I say, I want to be like an
African war song.
A spiritual slave song.
A radical Public Enemy song.
I want to be the expressions of what is
and what will be, I wanna be lyrical
Explosions of new blues rap music.
I wanna be in the tradition of
long live the Kane, Follow the Leader,
My Melody, Rebel Without A Pause, Freedom or Death,
Stop the Violence, My Philosophy, BLACK STEEL
IN THE HOUR OF CHAOS. I wanna be a
prophet of rage (scientific rage)

In the words of Flavor Flav:
Cold Medina Boyeee!
I Wanna be medina, (People oriented)
I wanna be Them, They, Us, We, I , I and I
blackness, not as in down or decadence but as
in life, livelihood, as in things unseen.
In the tradition of us, of warmth.
In the tradition of love or the things
that I love (by) Amina Baraka.
In the tradition of suffering, struggling and
womanhood.
In the tradition of those after
Harriets, Truths, Assatas, Hammers,
                              (small pause)
You thought you won didn't you! Thought
You taken all our women, but before
you turn back and smile with evil pleasure
I yell

Lisa Williamson, Aarian Pope, Sheri Warren,
April Silver!!
In the tradition of all our women.
                              (pause)
You must be insane, I knew you like death,
killing and decadent shit, but you must be crazy!
(Sick) you thought it was over cause the 60's ended.
You thought you won cause you got Nigger
horses carrying your cowboy philosophies, and
negro presidents, (sicing) dogs on their own people.
It's not over yet!
The only dead things around here will be you.
You like bookless be bookless, be educationless
You be BMWED and IBMED! you want imperialism
You have orgasms in the face of
capitalism, keep all of that shit, And go to
hell with it!
I want to be in the tradition of workers and
fighters, I wanna be like Bob Marley, a buffalo
soldier, like Steele Pulse and rally 'round
the flag. I wanna be a reggae song, a
kilimanjaro tune a West African fighting song
on the Isle of Goree!

(In the tradition of all of us everywhere!)
In the tradition of Niggers and Latin Americans,
Niggers and Puerto Ricans, Niggers and West Indians,
Niggers and Cubans, Niggers and Australians
and even Niggers and Europeans.

You thought you split us up, kept us apart
Ignorant and separated you crazier than
I thought. Take Louis Riveria, Pedro Pietri, Cheryl Byron,
George Xiegron, Willie Perdomo, Derrick Angellenti the
Puerto Ricanist Nigger
I ever saw.
In the tradition of common people.
In the tradition of socialism, Pan Africanism,
and peopleism. I wanna be like a Césaire poem,

an Ousman film, a Baraka play. I
wanna feel like the souls of a thousand Black folks.
I wanna be a Bambara, a Morrison,
a Sanchez, an Amina, I wanna feel like
a Hughes, a Baldwin, a DuBois
(I can name for days)

Sorry America, Europe, Western World
only thing you got is what you stole
and can't even perfect that.
Sitting big in your money filled lazy
chair wearing the crown of imperialism watching
your plague destroy the world! You will die!
You will be crushed and overthrone by those
who came after, those who you kill, and those
who came after them (the more you kill the
more we come) You will fall trust me,
take my word those in the tradition of
morals and life, those in the tradition of progress
and love will seek your doom to
the outer edges of the universe and you can't
even be saved by your mindless,
gestapo, white domes in Black face!
(Negro people)
In the tradition of youth and children
of Amiri's and Ahis, and Shani Baraka's. She
will slam dunk your very essence in
the hoop of eternal damnation.
In the tradition of Obalajis, Veras, and Wandas
In the tradition of family and togetherhood.
In the tradition of prophets and new generations.
You thought you stopped it all! Broke
down all forms of resistance. Fattened your
being off our souls but before you speak
with delusions of sanity Remember
H.U. take over '89 (The people united will
never be defeated) You will never escape it!
We will sit in, stand in, fight in, die in,
and even kill in.

I wanna be about those who were lynched.
I wanna be about those who were enslaved.
I wanna be about Eleanor Bumpers and Michael Griffith
I wanna feel for Tawana Brawley and Howard Beach.
I wanna be just like Larry Davis.
I wanna be in the tradition of those that were
murdered for our name   sake
Remember Malcolm, remember Evers, remember
King, remember Lumumba, Hampton, George Jackson,
And remember those people who you don't remember who
was victimized by this shit!
South Africa still ain't free!

In the tradition of Intelligence and leadership.
You say we ignorant, you know it all.
I say Nkrumah, Lumumba, DuBois, Amiri
shall I continue or did you have enough! Malcolm,
Martin, Farrakhan, you think that's it check out
Shameen Allah, Haqq Islam
Kevin Powell, One Hundred Black men of Rutgers,
Webbs, and Sealys, and Nia Force
Don't forget Allens as in Harry Allen
Media Assasin he will shoot down
your historical language of lies and
substitute it in redefinition of self (real self)
In the tradition of those who will come after.
In the tradition of new renaissances and
new revolutions, in the tradition of building
and power gaining. In the tradition of self-
determination. I wanna be
nobody but self.
In the tradition of my people. The only
people who will fight for all people.

I thank you. I thank you all who came
before us. I thank you Amiri Baraka
may blues people stay in our hearts
forever! In the tradition of your tradition.
May every one of your books be read in

the institute of Pan-Africanist thought. I
thank you for fathering me and marrying
Amina (my mother). I thank you and love
you in the tradition of all of us everywhere, in the
tradition of blackness everywhere, of peace everywhere
       I wanna be blackness, I wanna be peace.
I wanna be Amiri and Amina too. I wanna
be both of you! And I will carry the
tradition on in good times and bad and build
and create, create and build, build and create
create and build.........
          THE KLAN WILL DIE AND
      BLACK PEOPLE WILL BE VICTORIOUS!▲

Paul Beatty was born in Los Angeles in 1962. Had to leave the house in 1980. Went to Boston. Stayed there seven years, got two degrees, a mild concussion, and amassed a sizable debt.

Left Boston in 1987. Went to New York, been here since. Ready to go back to L.A. First volume of poetry, *Big Bank Take Little Bank*, was published in 1991.▲

➤ *Gription* ➤

wuddup
whaz hat-nen
you man

       two nigguh
       hands swing

in mid arc
fingers hesitate
wait is he bringin
that ol school soulshake
or he gonna skip step 2
do a quick slide n glide
           hope he dont trip
           and go into
           all that post grip
           flip wilson
           royal order of the
           water buffalo shit
        finger snappin
       hand clappin
     elbow taps
twists

then i'll improvise
my handshake guise
and just bang fists▲

➢Doggin the Rockman➢

ssssssoundcheck
onetwo onetwo
my boy elroy
suicidal drumtech in full effect
son of jane
and george jetson

miscegeny creation of hanna barbaric
claymation science

caught up
in Bedrock
frankenstein chemical compliance
all the worlds a cage
white boy mind trapped in black
body rampage
on surfers sabbatical

oh wow radical
im stoked
and fuckin bummer man
im broke

overfed hybrid
jazz drummin skateboarder
sittin in at club l.a. disorder
at the mid point of his
1000th bo joint coastin down a
hallucinogenic
skate ramp
here go
boy elroy
jettisoned into

backside air
tricks
acid trips handplants

fakies smack into
basehead tic-tac-politics

                              ask not what crack can do for you
                                    ask what you can do
                                            for crack

say a prayer for dead presidents
lincoln kennedy ford

dear lord
skateboard me not into
the temptations

if i have to beg
plead for your sympathy
i dont mind cause it means that much to me
aint too proud to beg baby baby
              mo bounce   to the
                              8th of an ounce

self-respect
smoked up
in quarter breaths

                              full rest-stop   death

                              pump-up the volume
                                    listen to a musician
                                          play musical chairs
switchin places with his
  teddy bear
                    and snare drum
here it comes

my man   runnin through damns
              and three and a half grams
alone in his room
naming that tune

damn i can match that first high
in one more hit

fuckshit guy
iiiiii   cant quit   im a hype

        dammit who in the fuck superglued my lips to the pipe

                        chill out homey
                        you aint no head

you not the type
                                got a bed
                        you fed
you aint sold
                that wack crackerjack gold chain

we macked to a lame fish
with a hook in its mouth
                        yo its same-oh same-oh
                        everythings cool
                        you still in the water
                                and surfers rule

        crack keeps bitin the dollar
tend to stay optimistic
   when yo nigguh wearin the collar

no one heard
                elroy jetson holler
                                                when he spent
two fifty for rent
to get bent

                borrowed two fifty more

                        borrowed another two fifty

on two dollars and fifty cent

could see six flicks
on one pink ticket
                              we snuck in every show
                    eatin popcorn yellow rocks
with no butter
                    on the fluffer nutter
                    nabisco nights
                    we left behind
                    the triplex
kung fu fightin
each other to fake deaths

                    boy elroy
beatin his own ass

badly dubbed
shaolin priest
kickboxin in his head

                              you killed my family
                              you bastard
                    todays the day you die

popeye the
hawaiian-negro sailorman

                                        toot-toot
who had fought
in the coke wars   couldnt stanz no morze
                    poured spinikch
                         down elroys throat
                              sang him the songs
                                   of nigguhs drowned
                                   on the d.c. PCP loveboat
told him
next time you dance
to the rock mix
                    think of the jimi hendrix experience

excuse me while i kiss this guy
popeye

the sailorman
                              saved him from the garbage can
                                          toot-toot
no more dependency fucks
with the goon
                              under the rockhouse moon

tama drummin his new beats
i can hear me n elroy
                                          runnin the streets
                                    callin each other cuz
                              talkin bout how we never wuz
                        goin to smoke none of that
                  no one had said jackshit
                                          bout crack▲

➤ *New York Newsday: Truth, Justice and Vomit* ➤

with each subway rereading
of black n white
n red all over   mornin tabloid
                     summer crimes of color
                     emmett tills keloids
                                boil n bleed

screamin for the liberal application
of media mercurochrome
but the warnin label says
                caution: use only on occasion

when whites fire shots or
                buy funeral plots

                            if symptoms persist discontinue use
                            and call physician

and im still wishin the new york times assigned
war correspondents to the south bronx
                DATELINE MORRISANIA
                3 pinchee morenos under concrete
                street pretext of chain snatchin,
                capped uh puerto rican who was
                guilty of swooping a jeep doper than
                theirs. in what was was a wackass
                exhibition of the lack of inhibition
                that comes from 'i double dog dare
                you' nights parlayed into a four-wheel
                drive bravery cheapshot plot to follow
                him to the homestead

then homeboy said

                                    gimme your chain

        and the muzzle nuzzled
        gainst his hypothalamus said

or i'll kill you

before he could reach for the clasp
        the puneta mega-
                    blast sent him into sub-
        sonic convulsions
                    in the repulsiveness

                                        that a home run away
                        892 bald
                        baseball
                        hot dog eatin
                        beat writers

watch the yanquis play
                a stadium game

                        where quitters never win
                        and winners never quit

                        and on the other side of the fence
                his pallbearers
        still cant believe this shit

where are the articles
        op-ed obituaries of contemporary civic shame

                                about how their boy caught
                                the atomic particles
                                of the shot heard
                                around the block

                with its bing bing bing ricochet
                ortiz funeral home tinnitus

                        deafening the hearts and behinds
                        of a daily circulation of millions

to the hazy

uniquely asian sound
of 100,000 murdered dry-docked hiroshima carp
flip floppin on the radiation hot plate of hate

the embalming starts in five minutes

so tap the ear

in which you hear
the air raid siren of race fear

lallygaggin n skippin
underneath schoolyard hopscotch sneakers
laced on colored crayon crane feet
that click   over sixes

land on one leg and kickstart the gong
with the other

smotherin recess with radio remix sutras
disguised as buddhist prayers
for the hearing impaired

red rover red rover
let the media come over

with redlight
greenlight quickness

fight fight
a nigger and a white

fight fight
a puerto rican and a mohican

whos through with watchin ultra chic
tv anchorgeeks

play cowboys and everybody else

in western repeats
where reporters run
duck duck
who gives a fuck circles
    around neighborhoods
      where hokeypokey is broke and they dont fix it
        unless they find oil on your property

   you put your right foot in
   you get your life took out

while the see no evil
eyewitness news crew snooze as

sioux kill mandingos

                  mandingos zing cubans
                    cubans pop rastas
      rastas skin dominicans

and everybody burned the jews   ring around the rosie
      pocket full of posie
   ashes...
   ashes   we all fall down▲

➤ *I Know You Are, But What Am I ?* ➤

yo black
      stay Black

     wine ease
     electronic japan sleaze
     bourgeoisie dirty knees
          look at these
          lip prints in the mud▲

Leticia R. Benson was born May 24,1963 in Houston, TX. She is currently living in New York City because she felt a serious connection after visiting that magical metropolis on her 21st birthday. She has a BA in anthropology from the University of Oklahoma and is working on a book of short stories and poetry.

      "Peace and love to my ancestors...at this point my writings seem to be from folks who have yet to be heard...cultural documentation is very important for history's sake...support all Black arts so the truth can be told...love is revolutionary..." ▲

➤*Asante*➤

(for: Sterling Brown, Henry Dumas, Langston Hughes,
Amiri Baraka and Quincy Troupe)

Seducin me
with yo loud ass
thoughts
Knowin i needed
all
of what
u   got
ta get   through
the heres

           nows
                & will bes
If ida known what was commin
ida belted
        buckled
                &   bolted
thisself
so far

          down...
till no sonnet
            sestena
                or soliloquy
coulda pulled
             me up
Had ida knew
sweetness came   in
haiku-n-free verse flavors
ida found the candyman
way way long ago

Temptin me
with neological images
Rhymein phrases
fulla: bloodwarmin
                spinetinglin

tearjerkin

motions
(mysterious lyrical stanzas)

Sweet bad
soul-clinchin
conductor #1
i dream of boardin yo poetrytrain
ridin through
                    ballad towns
blues counties
                    & couplet cities
Leadin me
                rhythmically on
Latherin me
                graffiti literary style up
Layin me
                poetically down

SHAME!!!
SHAME ON YOU!!!
(but do it to me one mo time)▲

➤ *The "P" Word Poem* ➤

Inside my ears
I built 10 inch thick cement walls
Then padded it with fluorescent purple carpet.

I took an eight inch ice pick
gouged both my eyes out
                    then
flushed the membrane down my toilet.

I gave myself a lobotomy
drilled a four inch hole
in the top of my head
                    then
scooped out my cerebellum.

With a West Indies machete
I chopped down my heart
                    then
squeezed it into a pulp of watery mush.

AND STILL!!!

I heard: "Nana? why mommie ovah there killin people
...ain't God gonna be mad at her?"

I heard: "Say Jimbo...whatsa darkie who becomes head of
the U.S. defense department...a nigger... a huk huk!!! ain't
thata good one."

STILL

I saw: mutilated Emmett Till's
                    gunned down Phillip Pannell's
                    wrongly imprisoned Clarence Bradley's

Minus a brain and a heart
I still knew pain: Yusef... PAIN!

Apartheid... PAIN!
Ethiopian... PAIN!

"Let's hate Black women 'cept Whitney Houston"...PAIN!

"Let's only love European aesthetics"...PAIN!

"Let's hate Black men 'cept Michael Jordan"...PAIN!

"Daddy who was Marcus Garvey?"
"Uhhh ain't he tha one usta run that liquor sto"...PAIN!

FOR COLORED GIRLS WHO HAVE CONSIDERED SUICIDE
WHEN THE RAINBOW IS ENUF...PAIN

INVISIBLE MAN...PAIN

AFRICAN GENOCIDE BY ANY MEANS NECESSARY...PAIN

"Mommie is my hair evah gonna be pretty like my barbie dolls?"
"Mamma praying bout it everyday honey but if it don't happen...
well we jes gone buy ya some"...PAIN

RED   WHITE   &   BLUE   PAIN

"Niggahs go back ta Africa!!!...Niggahs go back ta Africa!!!...say
Jimbo ya got ya Eddie Murphy ticket yet?"
"U betcha he's awesome"...PAIN

PAIN

              PAIN

PAIN

P - A - I - N

pain.▲

Charlie R. Braxton (1961-) is a Mississippi-born poet, playwright and journalist whose work is steeped in the rich fertile soul of the Blacksouth working class. He began writing seriously as a student at Jackson State University, where he co-founded Black Poets for a New Day, a writers workshop for student and community writers. He has read and performed his poetry at various churches, festivals, rallys and universities throughout the Blackbelt South.

Charlie is the current editor of *Informer Community News-paper* and a contributing writer to *African American Magazine*. His articles, reviews and essays have appeared in the *Jackson Advocate, Unheard Word and Hub City News*. In addition his poems have been published in *Black American Literature Forum, The Black Nation, Blues Quarterly Review, Candle, Catalyst, Harambee Flame, Massife, San Fernando Poetry Journal, Minnesota Review, Panglos Papers, Prophetic Voices, Sepia Poetry Journal* and *Thunder & Honey*. *Ascension From the Ashes*, his first volume of verse, was published by Blackwood Press in 1980. ▲

➤ *The Arts Are Black*➤

(And coming back!)

heavy hippity hoppity hipster
super duper do-rag wearing city slicker
most newly crowned greaseless prince of
pomade waves
yea
you
the hooked nigga with the def moves
from foolsboro u.s.a.
big mouth rapping funky toes tapping & shaking
your hips ass & arms
all the way down wall street
to become what
a madison avenue third rate original
stolen straight from the streets of harlem
and conveniently reproduced in the glamorously
stilted studios of hollywood
singing:
          "FAME! I wanna live forever
              I wanna learn how to fly........"
highballing on cocaine dreams & fool's gold
while the real world
turns to the dawning of a new day

(CUT!/
 all quiet on the set!)

remember
the days when
our artist were real
(poets/prophets/guerilla word warriors/
 camouflaged gurus)
audaciously declaring the sunset
of imperial doom
on the new horizon
of a people's revolution

yea
we took our art/ culture
serious back then

remember

back when
black was beautiful
and awareness (of the fact)
was a hip thang
pushing all power
to the people's consciousness
today
our culture has been captured
& caged in tin cans
pressed in/to celluloid exploits
& flashed before a silver screen
for all the world to see (& do)

but
(to the living)
CULTURE IS A WEAPON!
it comes constantly from the people
and all the white boys
on wall street and madison avenue combined
can't top/stop
the bombs & bullets
hurled
from the suffering soul
of a real black artist▲

➤*Apocalypse*➤

across the sandy dry plains

of the good old wild wild west

the thunderous din of dead buffalo

hoof beat out a desperate warning

to one and all

beware

beware

beware

jesus is a big mean assed black man

painted smokey grey

and boy is he mad upset pissed off

dressed in a camouflage shroud

a three day beard and packing

a steel blue jammie

last seen kicking asses

and calling names

headed straight for the second

coming▲

Nicole Breedlove 21, born and raised in the Bedford-Stuyvesant section of Brooklyn, NY. When I was 19, I joined a young writing group. Because the group fell into the 'art for arts sake only' trap, I decided to venture into art for the liberation of oppressed people. Currently, a liberal arts major at Borough of Manhattan Community College, I have performed, among other places, at the Village Gate, The Brooklyn Academy of Music, New York University and in Boston at the Audre Lorde "I Am Your Sister" conference.

I have had articles in *Outweek, The Village Voice* and *Vanity Fair*. I have appeared on PBS for the "Words In Your Face" series in 1991. In 1992, the independent small press, Kitchen Table Press, owned and operated by women of color, published a chap book series with my poetry group Nia Kuumba. "You had the strong Black male writing movement during the Harlem Renaissance. You had the strong Black male poetry collective called "The Last Poets" in the late Sixties early Seventies. Well I am part of a strong Black female movement, the forgotten poets!"▲

➤ *Black and Divided Or Chittlins and Caviar* ➤

Your Family:
Dreads
don't look good
with mink
Fights
with people of color
for people of color
to come of power
And when you do
you're looked upon
as too black
too progressive
(Next time
don't support
Aunt Jemima's relaxer!)
My Family:
we don't vote —
we survive
it's part of the game
Politics
aren't compatible
with Welfare!▲

➤ *The New Miz Praise De Lawd*➤

wade in the water
wade in the water children
wade in the water
God's gonna trouble the water
Hey y'all I'm Miz Mary but peoples call me Missy
cause they say I never miss the point
I'm also a God-fearing woman I mean I pray and things
are alright by me...Now don't get me wrong I ain't blind
I know God only helps those who helps themselves.
I also know that Jesus was a black prophet who was lynched
by Roman soldiers 2,000 years ago! (Now even I knew since I
was wee old that ain't no way a man could live during that
time in that heat and have white skin, blond hair and blue eyes).
I don't want nothin from nobody and I don't owe nothin
to anybody but the good Lord above. The bible say, "Whatsoever
thy hand findeth to do, do it with thy, might;"
Ecclesiastes Chapter 9 Verse 10! Thats why I give praise
everyday God gave us Larry Davis, Malcolm X and Steven Biko.
I don't believe in the Dream Martin had that Blacks are suppose
to be meek and abide by the Bible. I agree that his bringing
together blacks for freedom by way of religion was a good idea
but I think we've been obedient for too long. Now I know I
just said I was a God-fearing woman and I know that the Bible
says to turn the other cheek but Lord...that one has been
slapped too! I don't never propose violence but seeing what's
happenin' to young black people and older black people and
poor black people everywhere, an eye for an eye and a tooth
for a tooth is becoming more appealing as I grow older!!
wade in the water wade in the water children
wade in the water Missy's gonna trouble the water... ▲

Sonya Brooks, 24, was born in Berkeley, CA and received her B.A. in English, Magnum Cum Laude, from Spelman College in 1989. A performing poet and writer, Sonya was a winner of the Zora Neale Hurston and Langston Hughes Creative Writing Award in 1989. She has performed for such writers and activists as Toni Cade Bambara, Angela Davis, and Alice Walker.

Currently, a resident of Richmond, CA, Sonya has performed her poetry and others at local cafes, colleges and theaters throughout the Bay Area. She is now teaching creative writing, English A/B, and math at Arrowsmith Academy and encourages her students to display their creative talents. Her works have been published in *Catalyst* magazine and several college newspapers. ▲

➤ *Middle Passage* ➤

Chained bodies
Cramped spaces
Broken backs
Bent necks
Babies thrown overboard
                        Over 50 Million killed in

The   Passage▲

                        Middle

➤ *Untitled* ➤

Sweet molasses
rich chocolate
luscious caramel
so sweet
so tasteful
so good
sooo...
You, Mama▲

➤ *Grandma Talk* ➤

Ya say something botherin you...
Well, I hope it ain't money 'cause
I ain't got no money to put "gas in my tank."

I sho do hope it ain't "dofunny" 'cause
I can't come betwinxt no "bread and butter."
What is it chile? I ain't got all day, so
ya better shoot "straight from the hip."

If you got the "hibbijibbies," just pray
to the Lord for strength and understanding.

Chile, I don't know what's botherin you,
but whatever it is, always remember this,
"a closed mouth won't get fed." ▲

Gordon Chambers, a 1990 graduate of Brown University, is an assistant
editor, by day, at *Essence* magazine and freelance writer whose articles have
appeared in *Essence, Rolling Stone, The New York Times* and *Young Sisters and
Brothers.* By evening, he is a vocalist who has toured the United States and Japan,
appearing at The Apollo Theater, The Nuyorican Poets Cafe, Carnegie Hall,
Towne Hall, and The Public Theatre. As a poet, he has done readings at the
Schomburg Center for Research in Black Culture and Playwright's Horizon
Theater.▲

➤ *meditations on stevie* ➤

when I was a baby,
one of your many-mooded voices
rocked me to sleep
and sweetly caressed me
I was happier than the morning sun
when you sang about a peace that i could taste,
about "the visions in (y)our mind," and
when you told me you "could feel it in His spirit"
at three, even before I knew who God was, so could I

at seven
(when I woke up out of childhood amnesia
and smelled piss on my streets)
your other voice told me
that you wish *those* days would come back once more,
making me feel dark and lovely—
that gargantuan voice
grumbled and growled
"a child is born in smalltown mississippi,"
recounted, with conviction and sincerity,
days not forgotten when you, too, were livin' just enough
that proud voice that assured me that life for you
hadn't been that much a crystal stair
that you couldn't come down
and be with the folk that made you
the laureate that you are
your voice was like home,
and like me, was beautifully black.

at thirteen,
when i first started picking out
your elusive melodies
and unpredictable chords on my piano keys,
you dazzled my earlobes with subtle
segues from diminished ninths to
sharped thirteenths
and vocal runs configured

like's an architect's blueprint
but crafted and executed with the ease
of Motown choreography

and whether you pounded on that piano
with gospel effervescence
or tickled its keys
like the summer breeze does the bay
or when you oded aisha on the harmonica
with a couldn't-be-more-soulful-if-it-wanted-it-to solo
or when you improvised impromptu like the empresari Parker
and flirted with mistress jazz fascinating rhythms
on the horn obligattos of "do i do"
i heard a kaleidoscope of blackness
in the music of your mind,
a symphony and an opera
in the key of (y)our lives
i heard haunting melodies as perfect as sonnets,
homespun lyrics overjoyed with love for black folks,
and a spirit that would churn as long as i could hear.
and it was strong,
and it was tender,
and it was,
you and i

and we could feel it *all* over.▲

➤ *waxing poetic on Marvin* ➤

With each flowing pastel note, crowds swooned to the unmistakable
sound
Of his gentle tenor. They were tremlous at Madison,
mouths gasped, eyes anxious.

Heartbeats quickened pace
at the sight of the smooth brown face
and never-pompous smile,
Both in suit and tie, or jeans and tam, he was as cool as miles' mute.

The down-to-earth, soul-brother number one
Sang about sex and politics, unbothered by these polemics—

About intricate ghetto worlds, crying for recognition for legitimacy
His inner city blues made *us* want to holler,
and told us 'bout the goings on.

Sang about a trouble man, a would-be hero (if silver-spooned),
A soft-voiced, sweet-talkin', high-fivin' urban protagonist.

Like Wonder's misstra know it all, Marvin gave America's scapegoat a
voice.
His trouble man was proud, pragmatic, and prophetic:
   "three things for sure, taxes, death and trouble."

Seventies love songs had that carefree croon, that dashiki feeling—
That fuck racism and disenfranchisement,
let's forget 'bout America for a moment and,

Let's get it on! And Gaye, with funk-filled fender rhodes,
syncopated congas, lilting
   church riffs.
Falsettos nuanced with project romance, afro-freedom,
platform shoe power,
   and BlackLove.▲

➤ *if only for one night* ➤

Like a sprinter in a long-awaited race,
your impetus was forthright, but
quickly, surreptitiously
you were here, at the mark
But now, you are gone,
and soon, amnesia will resume,
and you will fade into memory,
into inkscratch in my ageless verse.▲

Tracy Clarke is a writer originally from NY. She spent seven months in Los Angeles working for a Black public relations firm. She has made a firm commitment to the arts which moved her on to Berlin, West Germany where she is now working as an editor/writer for a Black film journal for the "Seventh Annual Black Cinema Berlin". Currently, she is working on a book of short stories and co-editing a poetry anthology.▲

➤ *Will They Always Remember* ➤

rich night
sweeping out
the steam
blue
blues
i can feel it
this train
is bound for glory
black
blacks
faces in the window
too soon to rise and start again
black
black hands
with blacker circles
under the finger nails
i wonder when they last
saw their wives
swish
chug
swish
night train
takes their dreams
and keeps on chugging
a six month stint
two days for home
"Shhh, yes, now baby don't cry
it'll be alright...hush, now, hush"
"Come Bantu back to the train"
it rolls on
swish
swish
into early morning
we can stop this madness
Johannesburg
night train
swish

chug
chug
the sun rises over despair
digging black gold
down, down into chasms
of black money
the sun cannot rest there
swish
swish
chug
chug
listen
you can hear that train
black faces in the window
can only be silenced for so long
swish
chug
swish
listen▲

➤ *For babies unborn* ➤

give this to my mother
he said
to the white boy
and nodded
amerika has always triumphed over the poor
but never its own shortcomings
she hadn't wanted him to go...
oh, lord, jesus, look after my boy
ain't too many places a negro can go
with only a highschool education
and an easy smile
but uncle sam wanted him
the united states marine corpse makes men
and kills women and children
at least if we're on the same side, he thought
whitey won't be shooting at me
an M-14 pointed deep in the jungle
knows no color-except yellow
three months in...
no one told him he'd cry himself to sleep
or that he wouldn't be able to sleep at all
shit man
he whispered to the white boy
when we was in boot camp
i was all hyped up to kill
they took us out to the range everyday
but they ain't never had no targets
down on their knees begging for life
yeah man...
the black boy's voice trailed off
give this to my mother...
the small cross shone against the night
musta called him out
cause they shot him
pain ripped
bullet snagged
just under the heart

oh shit
shit
the white boy cried
and they shot him again
the white boy pushed back against the earth
he could smell wet leaves
and death
and shots rang out again
he reached out into the night
and saw the cross falling from
the black boy's hand▲

Michelle T. Clinton, poet/performance artist, was born in 1954, in Bridgeport, CT. "I caught sense of Berkeley & committed to the word in Los Angeles." *High Blood/Pressure* is her first volume of poetry. Her second book of poetry, *Good Sense & the Faithless,* is forthcoming. Michelle is a 1992 recipient of an NEA Fellowship for Creative Writing. In 1990, she received an American Book Award for editing *Invocation, L.A.: Urban Multicultural Poetry.*

about writing: "Word is vision & imperative. Politics is crucial to a functioning heart/body/self. Heart is central to a breathing politic."

about academia: i have no academic training as a writer. proud of that. because you can find the word, you can work up the voice & vision on your own, w/books & the mouths of people who read, as guides. ▲

➤ *Plan Of The Klan* ➤

How do you make a black man red
                    you bleed him
how do you make a red man black
                    you burn him

and what
do you do
to a jew▲

➤ *Warning To Young Bright Sisters/*
White AM. Culture 101A➤

Once, a pre-med white boy laced his fingers into mine
& introduced me to foreign films, espresso in cafes, & existentialism.
As far away from niggerism as I could get, I ran to him,
relieved to be caught by his thighs & fucked,
dry, for hours & hours & hours.

Hardened black faces filled the ceramic cups
& picked up the tips he left. I brooded,
& after Camus had been exhausted I suggested
Ntozake, Jean Toomer, Baraka.

"Why are you so angry?" he told me, & dropped my hand
when black men passed us on the street;
"Where do these moods come from?"

His childhood of piano lessons & little league,
an occasional bloody nose & a fat idle mother
was a calm crack in the black rat faces that haunted me
at night. The fissure grew & grew by white magic,
white power I wanted to be swallowed & cleansed.

I told him about mine: 2 and one half rapes,
nigguhs cutting up my younger brother,
cardboard in the bottom of shoes when it rained,
& poetry books I stole from the library.
Fatigued, he poured French coffee, lit a cigarette
& picked up Sartre. "Strive to be positive," he told me,
looking up from his book, "or at least impartial."

Impartiality scalds the tips of tongues into silence:
I said nothing. The crude dry lessons of hot white men
can make you numb. Or spin in anger exponential to street abuse,
or thrash in dizzy shame of black innocence.
Impartiality burns blind in young white men who feel
the hope of Nietzsche, the power of privilege
& the servitude of women who want only to escape. ▲

➤ *I Wanna Be Black* ➤

It was a time, that summer '66
when it always be some brother on the corner
in a beret, a leather jacket, green army pants,
wantin' to know what was a young child like me
doin' out in the night,
didn't I know it was dangerous,
why, what would your momma say?

Before the red devils & bennies
I got ten for a dollar, before
I turned to Smokey Robinson & ripple wine,
or gettin' finger fucked in some garage
by some body with a dick,

all that summer, at night time walkin',
I got schooled by miscellaneous black nigguhs
gone caring & literate
breakin' down the community party line:

Nigguhs need to pick themselves up out the drug scum,
the numb come, up out the sphere of the white man's
life plan & history & logic & systematic self hate
for black & funk & nap & snap & pop & fuck & fun
& just 'bout most the best thangs folks love to do.

And these brothers,
these big brothers would walk me home
no matter how far, how late,
& wouldn't put they hands on me
& wasn't disrespectful no kinda way.

Then my titties started growin' & I realized
I could leave my glasses home: just squint.
& then it be just 'bout guaranteed
some fool would take me by the wrist
& lead me through the shifting dance floor
at fremont high saturday night sock hop,

& grind all 'tween my thighs a full three minutes
'cause I was starting to get cute.

For a while I got so preoccupied
I guess I didn't read no books,
& after the Hampton thang
I guess other black folks
didn't wanna read no more books neither
'cause all that politicizin'
was turning out to be dangerous
to the conscientious individuals of the race
(nigguhs gettin' shot up by the FBI & carryin' on).

Or maybe we just came to a time in history
when pussy was just plain better
or maybe wine was not sour
or the devils on dope smoother
I don't know
but seemed like everybody flaked at once.

Now folks don't know who's Ron Karenga
Fonya Davis, & if you say black panther
they think you mean animal
& all the negros in dreads & greens & reds,
all the socialistic lesbian colored girls,
they so far away from this Jheri curl,
this wild dancing pussy,
LA's Prince obsession & South African gold
strung 'round black necks,

it don't seem like it ever was
a functioning community,
don't seem like it coulda been more than a myth,
a wish, a desperate hallucination,
that black people could love each other
in the cool & dark of Watts America
1966.▲

➤ *Black Rape* ➤

I got fucked & it wasn't no thang,
just a trip 'tween a boy 'n girl,
some pussy & cock disease
colonized our bodies,
made him take me down in an alley,
the knife still in his hand.

Just some man-woman thang,
take it like a woman,
take it like a white woman
raped by a white man,
not racially related, not culturally relevant,
take it like a woman,
bitch.

'Sides, black men are under
a lotta pressure I'm told,
got good cause to act it out.
'Sides, black boys got decent
reason to explode so

I got humped by a brother
& the sickness sucked up my cunt:
I wished for a demented caucasian,
Give me a clean hate,
I wasted a wish to make the cock white,
make the swallowing a smoother acceptable
kind of political pain.▲

Kimberly Ann Collins, 28, considers Philadelphia, PA as a place where she was raised, and Atlanta, GA, where she attended Spelman College, as the place where she grew up. Kimberly's writing captures the essence of her realities as an African-American woman who absorbs the pain of her peoples' struggles and the complete exhilaration of their triumphs. Her efforts have earned her a bronze Jubilee Student Award for Literature, a 1991 Outstanding Young Woman of America Award and a grant from the Georgia Bureau of Cultural Affairs, which funded the publication of her first volume of poetry, *Slightly Off Center.*

Presently, Kimberly conducts creative writing classes for children in Atlanta, which helps renew her faith in a world that seems to have gone crazy. It is her hope that the words that help save her sanity will in turn show the people that, "we are in war time and we must rise to the occasion to save ourselves and the playgrounds for the children yet to come." ▲

➤ *Sisters* ➤

Remember when
I came to Chadwick Hall
in zombie form
after catching steve w/
another woman &
you lit a joint
passed it to me
while I was still tasting
my tears &
we ended up giggling our asses off

Remember when
we stopped at Woody's steak shop
w/ a 1/2 pint of Seagrams
& you listened to me
analize and philosophize
about why
I'd rather be a writer
than a lover
& you tellin me:
"that's it
get into your writing"
while you knew full well
I'd fall for love again
I was jus' hurtin' a little
right then

And no matter
how sleepy
you'd always talk
to me at six
in the morning
telling me to cut the crap
& speak my mind
'cause you knew I never
got up that early

So when you told me
you called this morning
wanting to tell me
love #1 got married
& although you knew
it wouldn't be you
somehow
it numbed you anyway
I really was sorry
I wasn't there

And probably
if anyone were to read this
they would dismiss us
as druggies
not knowing that
through all our pain
it was you
& me
that brought us through
and we really can't
expect anyone to understand
that you &me
are sugar-blood
always
       gonna be
         sisters▲

➤ *I Am Africa* ➤

It is not
the Afro-
      centric garb
I may don
     or
the complicated twist
    that
may adorn my head

Africa is in me
    &
I am of her

Sometimes
    when walking
concrete sidewalks
    &
Pebbled beaches
I feel her snow white
       grains of sand
   seep&
      sift
between my toes
She is always with me

Africa is more to me
    than a token of affection
hung
    about my neck
worn
    to appease
the arrogant few
who associate
       or disassociate
according to how I appear to be

Africa is me

I am Africa

She is nestled deep
                    under my left tit
forcing me
                    to give rise
to those who
separate
            & desecrate
brothers or sisters
            who
choose to dress
        as they wish to
giving into
            variety
not
        ideologies

Africa is in me
        my walk
         my dance
          my lyrical way of talking
is all
        by way of Africa
&the
        kinky kinks
                that dress my head
whether straighten
        or natural
are part of my gifts
   given by her

I don't have to wear Africa
        if
I don't want to
        because
I am Africa▲

➤ *Trio* ➤

Listenin' to that
funky bass player
toe-tapin' piano man
vein-poppin'
        soul-thumpin'
drummer
        takes me back

Back to sassy
        jazzy sounds
sultry
        mind-feedin'
sounds
comin' from those juke joint
        finger-poppin'
times

Times when grandma
coleman
cabareted through friday
went
to church on sunday
still singin'
        "ain't nobody's business if i do"
watchin' bass player
closed eyes rollin
        'round
            &down
hummin' to the pluckin'
of his bottomless sound
        turnin' me back

Back when
        hogmaws
            chittlin's
&black-eyed peas
w/ louisiana red hot sauce

made for a lip-smackin'
    feet kickin'
eatin' good time
seein' piano man
substitutin'
his feet
    for what his playin'
hands can't do
usin' an elbow hit
    to keep the rhythm flowin'
moves me back

Back into
    smoke-filled rooms
double hands
    bangin' out rag time beat
seein' visions of lady
    singin'
      'bout strange fruit'
& a light-skinned chorus line
    in cotton clubs' harlem
feelin' drummer man's
    sticks
       snap
         &clap
clashing jazz
    & ancient congo pulsations
to create rhythmic vibrations
throws me back

Back when
    the copasetics
did it with their feet
    louie
with his horn
&dunham
    with sugar hips
Jazz
    that infinite

free spirit in loose clothing
Jazz
      afro-american
do
      bop
taking a time capsule
back
      back to where it all began▲

Lorena M. Craighead, a 24-year-old Detroit native, currently lives/loves/teaches/learns in Brooklyn, NY. For the past several years she has taught junior high and high school as a founding corps member of Teach for America. Lorena claimed poetry as her weapon of choice ten years ago and continues to "oil her guns." As a student at Spelman College, she was influenced by the self-empowered community of women like Judy Gebre-Hiwet, Gloria Wade-Gayles, Pearl Cleage and Sonia Sanchez. She continues to travel and read with several well-respected Blkpoets. Her work has appeared in *Focus*, *Word Up: Black Poetry of the 80's from the Deep South*, and *The Source*.▲

➤ *whole truth so help me God —*
also known as the gettin' rid of nigguz business➤

so here comes this mf (excuse me)
4 days too late
as if we cared or remembered where he was
...had some ole stale Easter candy
and blue eyed buttermilk Jesus type shit for the kids
to make them 4get too
he got mad when i told him clearly to
TAKE HIS SHIT AND GET
and stop trying to contaminate our family with his
inadequacies and sometime love

"Is that when the incident in question began?"

that is when it began.
i don't remember most of it, but when Sorraih screamed
i realized that i had just hit the floor
i guess it had been one too many times for us all.

"What happened after that?"

i functioned in a haze, but i remember him
crying on his knees and wiping the blood from my temple

"What did you do after that?"

i don't remember getting up.

"Did you tell the police that 'he got what he deserved?'"

yes, i said that.
look, it is not my fault that the mothafucka didnt' even have
the courtesy to die outside of my house.
call it what you want,
i know i'm innocent. ▲

➤*a wo/man's voice must be heard*➤

(for the love of s.nazeema, a true survivor/woman warrior)

i guess it was because it was the first time i had been anyplace
by myself since my sister had been held hostage and raped and
beaten and sodomized for ten days by a man she thought she
knew all the way home my eyes bordered with tears anxious to
spill but looking lonely and afraid on public transporation is
never a good thing to do first i read akbar but for some reason
my mind kept wandering i dug into my bag and read some of my
favorite sonia and then the tears pushed for real and as i paused
and looked around me for a breather it was the faces of all the
men that were imprinted on my mind the ones who were on the
bus with me every day at that time the ones who undressed me
with their eyes the way they always do but today my city spirit
could not reflect confidence and courage my whole world was
different and i wondered how could the fathers of daughters
be so insensitive to the basic respect and fundamental knowledge of
women who let them forget that we were the essence of all humanity
it reminded me of the shock and sickness that i felt when i caught
that man on the floor across from my cubicle at the library he was
looking between my legs and jacking off security was no more
alarmed than if i had said what time is it and no more helpful than if
they wore no watch i felt molested just sitting there and i was no
virgin coerced into trust it was no use being so afraid i told myself
that fear is only paralyzing to its victims but my eyes they kept
trying to flow tears for fears and shivers of anger i made myself look
at his picture to see a demented soul personified and there were no
tell tale signs my sister is alive dare i say well and she is as strong and
beautiful as ever and the whole experience comes from the nightmare
of my tormented sleep into the innermost of my waking hours to
scream into the face of our loved ones and more terrifying than the
nightmare itself was is willl always be the fact that it is real▲

➤ Dancin' Our Lives Away ➤

i seen't dis papuh cup dancin' across the street 2day
    yeah, i wuz n dah ghetto an if it wuzn't a soul sistuh
    tellin' this story it wudda been surburbia
    but that's not my rap fuh now
sad but true u cain't even dance with the wind
    cain't trust nobody deze dayz
    b cuz sumthin will make'm turn against u
    lil papuh cup
n u kin be lieve me cuz ah seent it wif mah own two eyes
ah watched as yo instinct n riddims complement yo spression
    ah guess we wuz boaf caught up n duh moment
    it all seems so simple
    at leas' dats dah way dey make it seem
it wuz jus dat cho partnah lef u hangin
    swept yo graceful passionate steps
    n2 dah guttuh
    n wifout a secon' or backward glance...
it happens to the best of Us, believe me lil' cup
an' u no fo an instant mah stomach felt that pitfall thatchu
    must felt
    discomfort
    tension
nervousness an all
    fo a moment ah wuz dere wicha
    but only fo a moment
    an then u were gone. ▲

William T. Crawley III(LaTief KMT), was born in Newark, NJ in 1966. He is a 1989 graduate of Morehouse College where he received a B.A. in political science. He lives in Brooklyn, NY.

William's poetry was featured in the 1989 Edition of the Catalyst literary journal. He is a member of KMT Fraternity, Inc., the first African fraternity in the United States.▲

➤ *Poetry for the Goddess* ➤

African sister, standing there in her radiant beauty;

"Yo baby, whass yo name?"

See her there, long Nubian cornrows gleaming in a healthy, glowing shine;

"Yo baby, I wanna git to *know* you!"

Beautiful sister, with curves like the winding path of the Nile;

"Yo baby, you got a big, fat, juicy ass!"

Her teeth, pearly white, her skin dark as the night, soft as the earth.
Her breath, short, sweet, moist like the riverbed of the Congo.

"Hey slim, I got somethin fo you!"

Her nose, broad, smooth, the nose of Heshepsut,
not long and pointy, not long and narrow,
but wide, wide as the African Savannah.

"Yo baby, I got somethin you ain't never had!"

She hears the cat-calls, the drooling, quivering,
weakly composed lyrics formulated by lewd
intentions...

My Sister

Your Sister

Our Daughters

Our Mothers...

African Womanhood, Powerful African Women, Forerunners of

Humanity, Creators of Life, Strength,
and Health.

Beautiful being of Nubian pulchritude...
There she sat, waiting for her Egyptian Prince.
But before his arrival, the compliments...

"Fuck you Bitch, you ain't all that anyway."▲

➤ *Bud* ➤

Back in 1935
On a hot Sunday afternoon in August
In Cyprus Creek, North Carolina
My Uncle,
        Theodore "Bud" Coppedge
          wuz
           walkin
            from
             the
              front
               of the
                Lettuce Hall Baptist Church

And four of the Harris Brothers, in defense of their sister's honor
and virtue, jumped on Uncle Bud—with knives.

Too bad
      cuz
         Uncle Bud
          wuz
           sportin
            the
              latest Smith and Wesson (a gun with bullets).

After the smoke cleared and the Christians took deep breaths, and
Bibles fell to the red dirt of Carolina,
the only Tarheel left standing

           wuz
             Uncle Bud. ▲

Malkia Amala Cyril, born in Brooklyn in 1974, has been reading her poetry in the New York City area since the age of fifteen. Before graduating from high school in June 1991, she had read at a variety of colleges, performed at the Audre Lorde "I Am Your Sister" conference in Boston, at the Brooklyn Academy of Music Majestic Theater, and was a finalist in the Nuyorican Poets Cafe 1991 Grand Slam competition. Recently she has performed at Aaron Davis Hall at City College and at Rutgers, Vassar and Hampshire College.

Malkia is currently a member of a poetry/performance collective of women of color called Nia Kuumba. They believe in using their creativity toward personal and collective freedom. In the fall of 1991, at the age of seventeen, Malkia became a student at Sarah Lawrence College.▲

➤ *Just Because I Am* ➤

Who asked the sun to set in the evening?
or rain to drown my tongue my lungs are pain
and asked my father to come for me in scenes that never happened
a faceless misery in the midst of a past I'll call mine if I have
to call it anything at all.
I'm Black and Brown and Yellow and Red. I grow in my mother's
garden
the flowers of youth dripping bloody sap onto my steps
and we fall together in a medley of tortured voices
screaming I am! I am! to each other, proving our existence.
And He watches like the evil twin of somebody's Great White Hope
though which is better I can't discern
and tides and tides again wash our dirty laundry
and media lines hang it out to dry
like coons on t.v. and white men in blackface miming the
distortions of their violent victories.

When the statistics come out alcoholic, wife-beating, child
abusers, drug addicts, welfare recipients, in jail, dead, they know
we have listened and believed them their lies.

I snap my fingers, sing Do-wop on street corners with the men;
my rememory is alive with moments like these and others live
fiercely in my history
workin' like Black sisters, or Black boys on the court
with a ball, a radio, a death kit, quick fix, glass dick defining
their manhood.
"I *am* a man" my they say with fists clutching fury coming down on
a pretty brown head.
"I *am* a man" my brother tells me with his hand on his dick,
afraid it'll hang with his body, limp and lifeless next to the
American flag, in the American way, shining keep our country pure
a.k.a. KKK just because he's Black.
Who was Robin Hood robbin' back in 1492
when Chris sailed the ocean blue to slice him up a jigaboo
I say where is my country now?
Who was the rich and who was the poor

now who cleans the floor and holds open the door and got to have
more than we ever had before?

Conceived as I was by a woman again I am born into another woman
for daily do I become new.
I am born into sluts, into bitches. I am born into hating myself.
I am born into confusion.   I am born into loving. I am born into
Audre's woman who needs without wanting and is dangerous.
I address the blood that flows from my womb (not baby-holder, not
microwave, not yours)
It reminds me of the sun when it pours into me and dreams me
daytime dreams of the me inside of me.
The well of loneliness is real and easy to call gay, but it's human
and it's mine night by night day by day I'm living with the pain
of loss.
Her lips are full and swell like the sea in a torrent of salty
waters and years,
my victories can also be my fears.
Because I love and make love with the passion of my youth,
the bitterness of lost naiveté, the bubbling anger of a thousand
suns exploding into the most blinding light,
I am woman and greater than woman
loving women is as ethnic as my skin, as mysterious as you make it,
but it's mine because I claim it;
and even sliced up, or crowded in by your definitions
will I be Black and love women till I die
will I be female and make love like an Amazon
will I be young and mistaken in my definitions
will I be a bridge over someone's troubled waters
will I be a wild woman swimming in the majesty of my future.

Complete and yet divided, I am more than the sum of my parts.
Don't pretend to understand me. There are crevices so deep that I
question their validity and their existence.

The world falls down around me in a crowd of questions
and preconceived notions about my life, my politics, who I sleep
with Why..?

Why is your hair so curly, you Puerto Rican or somethin'?
Why you like girls? Undergo some severe radiation or somethin'?

    and the fists and the words that sting and burn open wounds

Whatcha do in bed with a girl?
Are you the man in this relationship?

    and the need to be left alone drives me into a panic,
    an almost crazed existence

Why do you believe in magic?
Why is your spirit so Black?
Why, little Brown dyke, ain't you white?
Why? Why? Why?

my heart replies, full with the love of a woman,
and my soul howls an answer across the millennium of years between
me and this world
and they sing together above the tortured voices, looking past the
hanging boys, the bleeding girls, countries where my soul resides,
the spaces in people's minds that I have occupied

I am, they say together, without pretense just because I am▲

➤ *Children's Games*➤

Bang bang you're dead fifty bullets in your head
Bang bang you're dead fifty bullets in your head
Bangbangyou'redeadfiftybulletsinyourhead

Africa's a far away land I've never seen
never heard of
Tarzan is my tunnel into this vast continent
vine to vine   limb to breaking limb
makes real reality   this Uzi this crack in my spine
up my nose the cocaine of New York is power and I sell it
and I sell it...
Rasta vibrations yeah dreadlocks is a cult movement
and I'm down back to Africa   home and home's no place
for a 90's American Black girl
these movements of empty rhetoric render the stolen child
gone...
If it's about power then I got it down
Uzi Black brother with a noose around his neck
white man on top fuckin' him over from behind
ain't that a blip...
Everywhere Every corner a fast food joint   a liquor store
every dollar spent flooding lands of death lining dreams with blood
Succulent appendages of thought lay wasted on the outskirts of
this town   while children laugh empty laughs
at mothers torn and battered vaginas
the roots of all beginnings
the canals of life lie between these tattered thighs.
Here is the river filling with women's blood–tears
yanked out of existence by iron hangers and welfare
prison contains the way America contains.
There is no difference in the sounds empty eyes make
the words they speak all crying for one day of life
to approach us with respect with dignity and pride
but the dollar bill stands tall...

Bang bang you're dead
                    fifty bullets in your head
        the power is empty rendering Brown children gone

Fifty bullets in your head
> Quietly hoping and searching jail cells of inclusion
> Yeah we're a part of the system
> like inmates are part of the prison
> convicted of the crime of African descent
> denied trial by jury of our peers

Bang bang you're
>   *dead*
> Gravitating toward the source of the fear
> growing closer to the root of this hatred of ourselves
> discovering how a white boy must feel
> knowing the strange texture of the power to kill one
> Brown daughter after another

Fuck the sun. This is a raisin in an oven
with gas chambers of ignorance turned up to kill.

Fifty bullets
>   *in*
>   *your*
>   *head*

Spreadeagled on the air i assume the position of degradation
while children Brown and children learning walk through
school halls hands raised guns falling out of their mouths,
their pockets, blood in their eyes
crack in their stomachs   need in their voices
treating life like a game like the toys they are trying not to be.
Bursting growing inflamed
rage is the perfect motive for murder
pain, apathy and desire force that trigger finger to jump back
and attack and we attack who we see in the mirror.
Back to Africa and I'm down to go home if someone can find it make
it real for me again.
Tarzan murders every dream I once believed in,
the seasons continue to grow toward death,
and young eyes turn to stare angrily and helplessly, vacantly and
hysterically thirsty and hated, but never satisfied.

Fifty bullets in your head
>   dead...▲

➤*Jump Black Honey Jump Black*➤

This is a journey into sight, sound, pain
the lives we all live and die away from
as we grow older
—a journey into movement begins here
      Hey
                nigger run nigger yo nigger what's up?
run nigger hey nigger yo man I got your back
Run nigger go nigger hey nigger go nigger
run nigger run niggerr Run! Run! Run!
yo————————————————-homeboy
homegirl
it's a prison term we servin'
a heavy weight boxin' tournament they got us playin'
That's how they kill us
it's a conspiracy, man
give that girl a run for her money
Corporate balls bells toll the tale
loud and clear ringing from here and there
I heard niggers got tails between their legs
      Playing basketball
      We're playing basketball
because boys will be who the world creates
after school after lives of love are over
they play
the court confines them—(this like jail man)
playin' ball like they leavin' the world behind
proud and strong
an' boys are boys and Black and red is for the blood we shed

I remember like he remembers sometimes the wind
the marshes beneath his feet
Girl, go on with your bad self
steppin' live livin' hard
it's a man's world we runnin', runnin' from
don't give him credit for what you done
you wanna sit back when he slap you?
Better 'kill him when he turn around. Believe it, believe Jesus

Thy Father who art in heaven can't remember who I am
but I remember the wind on my back
the daisies and good smells in her eyes
remember the heat...
October can get real hot if you let it melt
in Black and Brown this is a chocolate month when love begins
and we flow from the center
we are the core.
La cucaracha, we share our streets with animals
treated like yo man you act like I'm Black or somethin'
stepped on! kicked out, half starved, fightin' back
scared, alone hurtin' together with each other alive.

Hey girl, keep on steppin', the world's a crazy place
meanin' run nigger go nigger get away from here
waterfalls of my life cascading down
shrouded in elusive meaning
African dresses on tanned white skin
White boys are basketball stars, jeans falling, being held up by
leather instead of ass,
yo, be all you can be
but try as you might, you won't never be me.
Concrete livin' brownstone dyin'
Gentrification pushing us together
driving us apart don't know where to go
how to get there   running toward a mirage
thievin' our lives, stealin' our heartbreak
imitatin' what they created,
what they could not stop from being created
callin' it flattery...
Run from it all! the whispers howl
the dying the hatred the fear the sickness
the shots ringing out the tales of too many cities
the prison of Black lives
the imprisonment of my double heritage lover in a strange caste
system.
Lies lies in the beginning
              white is right and
then Jesus, Holy Jesus killing Black in dark alleys

babies bleeding out of wombs and lives and livelihoods
and straight A students and back seat Chevrolet babes
and forced Brown skin on pavement
livin' a concrete life is hard
and walkin' the streets might make me forget
but it don't make it go away
it never stops.
Then
      from sea to shining sea the blood wars rage
and they keep coming and blasting my definitions
right out of the water
and death is not the end of the game.
The shuffle gets quicker, the beats are faster,
the words are sadder because they mean nothing.
The clouds get darker, the sun shines brighter
and basketballs smash glasses and leave people
blind and they grow and it grows like a storm
that just won't blow over.
And the whispers howl white
run nigger, go nigger, go nigger run
Black eyes shine back the fun's just begun
                        yeah....▲

Thomas Sayers Ellis was born in Washington, DC and raised on Seventh Street, "A crude-boned, soft-skinned wedge of a nigger life breathing its loafer air, jazz songs and love, thrusting unconscious rhythms..." Mr. Ellis is a founding member of The Dark Room Writers Collective and an editor of its journal: *Muleteeth*. His poems have appeared in *AGNI, Callaloo, Hambone,* and *Lift.* Currently, he lives on a hill in Boston from where he has been able to achieve the necessary distance to watch DC like a hawk.▲

➤ *The Break of Dawn* ➤

Explosive posters lit at night.
On every tree, a cardboard savior
nailed to rooted echoes of wooden agony.

Sidewalks graffittied with chalk silhouettes,
stink of murder, scabs of moonlight
patch our wounded night.

Wrapped in bandaged blue, pale morning
wakes the day. Mute doses
of evaporating darkness on the breath of potholes. ▲

➤ Hush Yo Mouf ➤

(for Bob Kaufman)

1
Pretty soon, the age of the talk show
Will slip on a peel left in the avant gutter.
2
I refuse to write for more people
Than I can listen to.
3
I tripped over a tongue last night
And failed to wipe up the metaphors.
4
The world is held together by the word
Of one person who ignores everybody.
5
The Space Race is foolish;
NASA will never catch up with Sun Ra.
6
Since Virginia Beach, I've added Heckle and Jeckle
To my list of endangered mythical beasts.
7
My father and I have my mother in common.
She does all the talking.
8
A slap in the face is the most corrective form of punctuation,
Sentencing.
9
Bomb coffee houses, not abortion clinics.
10
The preachers of plasma say Give the gift of life,
Rhetoric.
11
Talk, talk, talk.
Lies, lies, lies.
12
A thousand pubic persons, all publicly pissant, politicians.
14

Talk, rumor, he say she say, word of mouth,
History.
15
WANTED DEAD OR ALOUD
Someone to rinse the tongue stuff from my eyes
16
I, too, write writing:
17
We bony V's
Trying to make a W.
18
And drink ink.
19
Child, please.
20
I came to this planet to escape walkie-talkies.
I failed▲

➤ *On Display* ➤

A Ghost with PCP eyes
Bops through my memory.

Her skirt rises, as she
Spins through love boat,

Lagerfeld & hot breath. *"Up*
Against the wall, standing

Very tall, he's got the big
Spotlight & he's doing it all."

We playact black ants surround-
ing a crumb, then go at her

Like a broken drum roll banging silence. Six, seven,

Nine, straight through her.
"Turn off the house lights ya'll,"

Says Jas. Funk, *"So we can put*
everybody on display.

Aw turn off the house lights
Ya'll, so we can get everybody

On display. Aw get it!"▲

➤ Making Ends Meet ➤

My mother made Big Macs & beds
While we sat home watching
Marcus Welby & Reverend Ike.
Years thawed
In front of our television set
Before we realized
Her hands were more important
Than theirs, before
The world around our own focused
And we were able to see through
The miracles of Palmolive & Bounty.
My father walked out the day
Carter waltzed in, shedding
A surface of wax,
& long before
My fear of him wore off,
The ghost of his love for soul
Came back, drifting
In & out of bedroom windows,
Whispering which sounds to record & why.
As if dead,
He explained how his world began
Where ours ended, breezing
Through a litany of promises.
He bought me timbals and blank tapes,
Hoping I'd look the other way
While he sped through walls,
Driving slow women,
And some nights I did just that,
Drowning out the sounds
Of mother & ghost
With strokes of my own.
Other nights I'd lay wide awake,
Recording every word
& before long
The ghost stopped coming,
But I kept going, purchasing

Value-Paks of Certron & Ampex
Instead of TDK & Memorex,
Praying the cheap cassettes
Wouldn't pop, ready to rehearse
My role as daytime
Doctor & God,
Forcing each end closer
Than the memory
Of parents kissing.▲

Joette Harland Watts (Kupenda Auset), 24, was born in Atlanta, GA. She studied at Spelman College under the tutelage of acclaimed poets/writers Pearl Cleage, Mari Evans, Gloria Wade-Gayles and Sonia Sanchez.

Still a resident of Atlanta, Kupenda has shared her essays and poems in gatherings throughout the South. Her works have appeared in various local and national publications. Kupenda is an aspiring educator of African and African-American studies, and plans to attend graduate school at Clark Atlanta University.

"The gift that comes through me is from the Most High. I am thankful." ▲

➤ *Let It Be Known* ➤

Let it be known that
you cannot make me
feel good, do a thing
for me, rock my world
or otherwise no matter
what the length of your
thing-a-ma-jig or
the tongue acrobatics
you manage.
know that unless there
is a balance between
your spiritual, mental
and physical and mine
too, your sexy body is
no more to me than a
dead corpse moving
inevitably, exhausting
its last breaths.
know that anything less
insults my womanhood
that includes any
suggestion to fuck me
remember that *if* all I
want is physical feeling
I can always pay somebody
to do the same thing and
trained, they'll probably do it
better/and *if* all i want is the
physical feeling, I can
go 15 minutes up the road
and buy an inexpensive
vibrator.
know that I get no thrills
from one night stands,
nor a continuum of the
same if there ain't nothing
more to it than being in

heat 365 days per year.
if, perhaps you find yourself
looking through an open door
which watched me leave without
your hospitable guidance
to it,
the whiff
of dryness you sense
is due to my steadfast
conviction
that there is
nothing more pleasing
than
substance.▲

                              ➤*re*
                              sist
                              con
                              fine
                              ment➤

when i thought about him
i said from now on i'm just
gonna keep my thoughts to mySELF
                              TO myself
                              to MYself

but it was too late cuz'
i've been calling it like
i've seen it too long

when they told me i had to
talk a certain way using
"standard english" i wanted
to know who set the standard.

"is you goddamn crazy" i asked
them out loud. "i done already
learnt enough about you to let
you tell me what to do"

so i told stuart if his strategy
was to play the game and not
believe in it, DO it.

he said what if i invite you to
a cocktail party at the bank—
what would you wear? i said
"irrevelent." i never said
i was going to bust up in ibm
nowhere with a dashiki on but
didn't say i wouldn't either.

we all need exposure

i'm not gonna accept
that's the way it is
and i said what i wear
to work, how i wear my
hair and how many earring
holes i got don't have
nothing to do with my per
formance

and he said but that's
how it is so i said re
definition and he agreed re
education

and i said it all over again
except what i said different
this time on a note i wrote in
his notebook was
"fuck white corporate america" ▲

➤*For a Woman's Rights*➤

For you, I cry this paper down into words on Black feminism.

For you, whose beautiful, Black, sacred womanhood has been snatched.

For you, whose "man" has taken the authority to play a male God; Omnisicent and Omnipotent.

For you, who is constantly watched, followed to work, even monitored while you slumber and only in your dreams do you dare ask "Ain't I A Woman?"

This is for you, who forgot how to sing but hums to yourself the words of Bessie Smith, "Yo' treated me wrong, I treated yo' right; I work fo' yo' full day and night.

This is for you, who tip toes through your house, beat down like the stump of a tree. While you are confined within his definition, occupying his space, going by his time, living by his circumstances—assailed, pervious, and destructible, you try to remember the words: "I am a Black woman tall as a cypress."

This is for his slave-woman who is raped and forced into the conception of his slave-child.

For you, who is branded by teeth marks in your skin from your "man" who eats away every day a portion of your spirit; a breath of your baby's life.

For you, whose veins bleed while you talk, whose eye swells as you walk up to the kitchen sink to wash his dishes in the dishwater that "back no reflection."

For you, whose "man" has chosen to decide if you will live or die, eat or starve, be broke or have wealth, be educated or uneducated, go out or come in, and most of all give birth to a live or stillborn baby.

For you, who lives each day with threats against your life and the precious life of a growing baby inside of you.

> For you, who only
> wants to be what you are
> You want to be a Woman.
>
> For you, Mother by force,
> African Queen by nature,
> and Sister by fate,
>
> I am your abolitionist
> by obligation
> knowing that my efforts
> today
> may be a day too late
> tomorrow.▲

Darryl Holmes, 34, was born in Brooklyn, NY and received his B.A. in creative writing from Queens College. He is an alumnus of The Afrikan Poetry Theatre In New York, and has emerged as a poet of considerable sensitivity. Raymond Patterson calls him a poet with unmistakable lyric gifts. He is the recipient of the Gwendolyn Brooks Award for Poetry and his work has appeared in *Obsidian II, Black Books Bulletin, The Small Press Reader* and *Essence.* His first collection of poetry *Wings Will Not Be Broken* was published by Third World Press in Chicago. *Kneeling Over Their Shadows* is the title of his forthcoming volume. Darryl believes that "poetry has an undeniable spiritual power to move."▲

➤ *We have never seen the sky light up* ➤

we have never seen the sky light up
look at the bombs
the children dancing out of their bodies
the dust from fallen buildings
birds coughing into broken windows
water running from everywhere.

imagine brides dying in their wedding gowns
joined to their father's hands
their husbands split in half
bleeding from a thousand places.

imagine running to hide in garbage cans
and subway stations
in barns or in silos
the military shutting doors
closing secret chambers
blocking the shelters.

the brooklyn bridge falling into the river
the faces in cars creeping toward death
drivers frantically spinning their wheels.

your mother's mouth floating out to sea
your semen burned
in the middle of ejaculation
a fertilized egg exploding inside the womb.

we have never seen the sky light up
look at the bombs, the stone
the powder and the paint
the walls crumbling everywhere.

look at the skies we light up in other countries
the skuds we conquer with our missles
the rice fields we've painted red.

look at the woman in kuwait
who only wants to know
when her laundry will be ready
when the sky will return to its natural color.

and our people are taught
to sell flags along the highway
to tie yellow ribbons around their favorite trees
our people are taught never to question
to accept the killing softly
to stand up for the home of the brave
and the land of the free.

and the man on the corner still shakes his cup
and rats still bite our children
and the women are still forced to bend over
and the air is still choking us
and aids is still killing us
and autumns are never promised to the poor.

look at the bombs
look at the men who denigrate the creator
look at the deals they cut
look at lumumba dying in the congo
look at allende being crushed
look at malcolm lying there
king crumbling on a balcony
fannie lou pressing the bubbles from her legs

look at queen mother moore
alma john
alice childress;
john henrik clarke
james baldwin
look at the poem in a young girl's hair
the homes we create
the kitchens we keep clean
the songs we sing on sundays
our suits

dizzy gillespie's cheeks
robin harris' eyes
george carlin's mouth
mick jagger's lips
stevie wonder's courage

we have never seen the sky light up
look at the bombs
imagine bush's tongue blown off
and stuffed in saddam's mouth
imagine them both taped to a rocket
imagine the rocket going off

look at the sky; applause spilling from everywhere▲

➤ *Tubman Strong* ➤

you never asked for sunshine
only shoulders to bear the load
a shout at the end of the tunnel

you never cried when they cut you
not like they wanted you to cry:
a simple woman song
a wail outside of your rhythm

something in the shape of a mountain you are
a mississippi crossing
a delta rock
something in the weight of a tree
watching seasons pass between your fingers

how many bails of cotton; how many pots
how many bedspreads folded
jars stuffed
how many illnesses without doctors
how many knocks at the door

how much water after the violations

how much soap

how much faith beneath the sun
under the whip behind the plow
over the wall through the fire

and you never cried when they cut you
never jumped up in the air
or laid down or crawled
not like they wanted you to

something in the mood of the rain
mixing with the earth
never crossing over

or calling God, out of name
never hurting your babies
or hungering for more than a chance
to spin until you dropped
to dance where the apples were falling

so many streams stuffed into one heart
so many plants and birds and forests
so many people fighting a war

and you never cried
or kept a rope beneath your head
never pushed your mouth into the water
or walked without your bones

you sang until the moon met you halfway
rose vertically in the air
out of your body
in the middle of the night.
you soared while sleeping there
you sang while the chickens slept
and the pigs rolled over
and the fields were still
and the men who struck you
fondled their bodies; fondled their guns

you gathered hisbiscus & honeysuckle
sprinkled red brick dust in the air
and you asked for extra skin over your knees
extra skin over your feet
extra skin over your hands

and you hung there halfway between
the moon and your window
halfway between a blessing and a curse
cupping your fingers
spreading your wings

and you never cried when they cut you

never jumped in the air
never pulled the alarm
never offered to scream

never ever offered to scream

not like they wanted you to scream

something in the sound of a river
something in all us we treasure. ▲

➤ *Nostalgia* ➤

I watched my mother at the microphone
her frail body vibrant again
her soft blue voice whistling steel.
so much strength, for a moment
the years beneath her eyes took wings
the curved roads of her life
came slowly together.

And my father took his place beside her
trying to remember the songs
trying to tell her he loved her again
that she looked pretty in her pink blouse
and plum skirt.

and although she didn't cook like she used to
maybe at night, after the family had gone
he would take her in his arms
and they would turn out the light together.▲

➤*A Time For Guns*➤
(in memory of Martin Luther King Jr.)

would I have marched with you Martin
moved to the color and cadence of your voice
rolled with your vowels into consonants
coming on like waves

would I have blown fire from these fists
faced the twisted mouths of murderers
turned the other cheek
as they chastised me with hose

nineteen years after your death
after they blew you from a balcony
and the butterflies fell from your bones
nineteen years after the earth stood still
and a movement staggered across America
the stones are still coming

the cries of Birmingham children
are broken by Atlanta
the blue sky is scarred with blood
and the bones of Eleanor Bumpers
are breathing for justice here Martin

would I have marched
knowing the faces you met
still move in Forsythe County
where klansmen demonstrate
against your holiday
knowing that Arizona is rescinding
her conscience
and Reagan is riding cavalry
into the hills of Nicaragua

I believe in mountaintops
in the blue water of our birth
in the brown bodies that built this country Martin

but we walk alone in our quest for peace

those in power do not surrender to spirit
do not meditate on trees or the fruit they bear
they believe in alternatives Martin
maybe it is time for guns...▲

Esther Iverem, born 1960 in Philadelphia, lives in Harlem with her husband, the writer, Nick Chiles. Her articles and essays have appeared in publications including *Essence, The New York Times* and *New York Newsday,* where she writes about community arts.

She has performed her poetry around the country and published it in journals including *The Nation, The Black American Literature Forum* and *The American Poetry Review.* Studying journalism and ethnic studies, she received her B.A. from the University of Southern California and her master's degree from Columbia University. Her forthcoming, first book of poems and photographs is, *The Time: Portrait of a Journey Home.*

Iverem (eeVEHrem) is a Tiv name meaning blessings and favor. She wrote in a recent essay to Malcolm X, "From this precipice at the close of the century, we either fall or fly." ▲

➤ *Journalist's Convention 1987* ➤
(For Idris)

Miami lights beckon,
gaudy in the distance,
like a nighttime whore.

No place is as lonely
as this rocking pleasure boat
filled with the brown and ripe
seeking pleasure.
No place has pleaded, screamed
as much for my touch
the touch of anyone.

But if Delaney, Césaire, DuBois
and Hurston could have touched it,
would they have touched it?
Laid hands on this still sinking abyss,
this empty pool filled with empty eyes
of those holding empty hands?

We wanted so much
to change the world.
But I have seen today
the world's best dancers,
their stuffing ripped out and trailing,
as they step right up to the block
to be sold: our modern-day auction
of meat above the neck.

And Aimé, I ask, for whose kingdom?
Who laughs at our race in continental drift,
dancing from winged apparitions of death's head.
Aimé, is this the legacy?

And you,
you strong and arrogant dancer,
check your centuries-old passport

check your shoes and canteen mired in seaweed
check, watch for chain-link leg irons
chasing your ankles like piranha.
We wanted so much
to change the world.

I see you
I see you
doing the shoulder-shaking limbo.
Toward the glittery city you go.

you go.
you go.

we go.▲

➤ *Faith #1* ➤
(For North Philly)

Protect the gleaming, battered soul of her.
Protect her with knives and flat, shiny fists
—at 23rd and Diamond where the only rain
has been the scabs of AIDS
—in some shrinking, shaking country
where the bone-thin blow
like dead leaves and blue wisps of hair.

In the murmuring and restless soil
beneath Watts, Haiti and Chad,
there are old bones from Benin.
There is Robeson with his arms stretched out,
holding one long, silent note,
that all screams and bitter wailing fall into.

Across every stubborn stubble of savannah
from the rat-driven dumps of Lagos
Solid, flat feet have still grown
like trunks of mahogany.

And her children spread out on the earth
With knives, with hammers, with light.▲

Trasi Johnson, born in Washington, DC approximately twenty-five years ago, is a graduate of the University of Maryland. Her work has appeared in *Callaloo* and *Muleteeth.* She is a member of the Dark Room Writers Collective. The most common statement made in reference to Trasi comes from her grandmother, Charlotte P. Johnson, a wise woman of the ancient sort, "Girl, you look like you combed your hair with an eggbeater." ▲

➤ *Until He Comes* ➤
(or ravings of a mad woman)

Plato was a fascist.
Freud was a nut.
They both hated women.

T.

Time and rhyme rhyme right,
But is a pillow soft?

The moon is dim, the sun is bright,
But does the pope wet the bed?

No, he's anal retentive.

T.

I was supposed to leave at seven-thirty,
But I woke up.

T.

Is love base ten or eight?
If I raise it to the power of infinity,
Will it equal zero or 42?

T.

Morality is slavery of the mind.
How pretentious.

T.

Men make the worst philosophers.
They have too many sexual hang ups.
Masturbation without guilt is the key.

T.

The world is microwave popcorn.

T.

Men are jealous because women get
More out of sex.
Ask Tiresias.

T.

Vaginapussysnatchcunt -

How can something so perfect
Sound so vulgar?

A man invented the bra.

T.

What *is* the price of tea in China?

T.

Your mouth on mine is like...
My mouth on yours.
Which is which?

T.

When he comes, will I come too?
It does not matter, sex is
More than that...

Bullshit.

T.

The universe is in the palm of your hand.
The lines are life and they never change.

                    T.

Being Black is a Big responsibility.
Being white is a drag.

                    T.

Fuck me hard, fuck me hard—
What does that mean?

                    T.▲

➤ *12 second poem*➤

If you
      my lover
want to drop a penny from the top of the
empire state building at a speed of 1200
0000 miles per hour and bore a hole in m
y skull seven and a half inches deep sev
ering my right brain from my left just t
o prove Galileo's theory then baby go ri
ght ahead.

                   T
             12 second poem▲

Ira B. Jones born in St. Louis, MO. Published in *Break Word With the World, Front Lines, Bop, Sing, Take Five Magazine, Wordwalkers, Catalyst,* and *Literati Internazionale.* A member of So What Performance Ensemble, The Langston Hughes Society and the Association of Black Psychologists. Presently working as a Habilitation Specialist with mentally retarded individuals in St. Louis County. Also, co-founder of the St. Louis Black Man's Think Tank and First Civilizations.▲

➤ *Echoes of the Murder of Emmett Till* ➤

1
white men are behind this night's door
knocking...knocking...knocking
with loaded gun in hand
flashlighting death between brown eyes bulging
staring...staring...staring

out of Uncle Mose Wright's courage
is Emmett waking into nightmared death
for whistling...whistling...whistling
at an ugly white woman in America

white men are searching...searching...searching

through his naked soul
floating...floating...floating
face down in the muddy Tallahatchie
Emmett's life tied to a cotton gin fan

his funeral procession
is an open casket
for the world to see...see...seee
white supremacy in his mutilated black face

2
is this trail over this faceless black body
wearing Emmett's initialed
ring...ring...ring
ringing of his death

while Uncle Mose Wright...Wright...Wright
sees them men
who knocked Emmett
into the night...night...night

3
"der he, der he"

Mr. Wright's ancient eloquence
shining light on

roy bryant and j.w. milam
smiling...smiling...smiling
into black faces
crying...crying...crying...

4
injustice...injustice...
in Money Mississippi

your voice...voice...voice
has not cleared my mind...mind...mind...▲

➤ *The Revolutionary Vision* ➤

The revolutionary vision
looks through the skull's eyeball into a new breed
As foggy spirits raise skeletons from past brighter days dawning
Bullets are screaming
Wake up revolution
so we'll all be there like gunfire
When the chickens come home to roost▲

Kim C. Lee, (Ngabile to those who know...) is a writer, educator and orator in process. I was born during a time of war, August 24, 1967, a warrior from the start. I grew up in Washington, DC, and am presently a resident of Atlanta, GA. I graduated from Spelman College in 1991, with a specialty in English/literature. This is my first publication outside of college journals. I am presently trying to make ends meet, but I am confident that things will come full circle. I plan to continue my education and am going for my Ph.D. in literature.

"I was raised on love and that loving fire has turned into a passionate flame that compels me to create. It is a blessing to share that love and every time someone appreciates my creations it's like passing a torch." ▲

➤ *Haiku #3* ➤

I have a friend who
calls me Butterfly. I guess
she's a collector.▲

➤ *On South Africa* ➤

How
Can You
Untie Your
Brothers' Hands
If Your Hands Are
Tied? ▲

Wil'um Lee Born in Coconut Grove, Miami, FL, poet-writer Wil'um Lee (Danny Bellinger) is currently a resident of Atlanta, GA. He is published in the *Catalyst* magazine edited by Pearl Cleage, the *Catalyst* student magazine at Morehouse College, Atlanta, GA, *Black Poetry of The 80's From The Deep South,* an anthology of poetry edited by Kalamu ya Salaam and *The Forum* newsletter of Clark Atlanta University.

Lee was enrolled in a poetry workshop under poet-activist-educator, Sonia Sanchez at Spelman College, fall 1989. He is also the author of a book of poetry titled *you can call me johnny taylor,* that he published in 1990.

He was a participating artist with the National Black Arts Festival, 1990, Atlanta, GA, "Literary Celebration/Publication in the Diaspora: Strategies for the 90's," poetry reading-Spelman College; Kingfest participating artist, "Lyrics To Live By/NBAF Day, 1990," poetry reading; book review in NBAF issue of *Catalyst* magazine, summer 1990. Lee has done numerous poetry readings on college campuses and various other places throughout the city of Atlanta.

Wil'um Lee (Danny Bellinger) is employed by The King Center in Atlanta, GA, where he is a reference assistant and apprenticing archivist in the library and archives, and he is also a graduating senior at Morehouse College class of 1992.▲

➤ *aunt martha* ➤

beer, malt liquor talks
slow...like billie holiday
fed her children peanut butter and jelly
sandwiches for dinner when they lived
in viet nam
apartments

she has seen better days

an affair with a prisoner
sweet talk him out of his money
two dollars at a time
kiss him and put something down
her bra—she was suppose to be visiting
her brother in law

she really enjoyed the place

had a baby at 44
who is the younger uncle of his older nephew

and the children, they play
bump heads and laugh
as aunt martha smiles...
with false teeth▲

➤*simple like that*➤
(for tonya, who thought burnt
coffee would be enough)

these words have no imagination
they are flat and simple
like the rusty brown hands that put the new
sole on my old shoes
the leather and shoe polish
smell that loomed in the air
the worn carpet
like the whole my big-toe was
finding its way through
the antique machines
that sucked sweat out of
the repairman's pours and the smell
of sweat and leather
together with the newspaper
i waited watching the ink
melt on my finger-tips
the newspaper the lady smiling
sat on

these words are simple like that:
you have not changed me.▲

Janice Lowe, born in 1963 in Cleveland, OH, studied creative writing and music at the University of Alabama and Berklee College of Music. She is co-founder of the Dark Room Writers Collective and has been published in several journals including *Callaloo* and *Muleteeth*. Ms. Lowe is a resident of New York City where she is a professional vocalist and songwriter.▲

➤ *Between Acts* ➤

this poem should have started
in the street
didn't even
check out the sky
or listen to
birds
in the chimney, didn't
meditate or sip tea
on Toni's quilt from home
aunt or grandma made
whoever,
choreographed
stripesdotsflower:

Art? i ought to hang this
could get lost in
redwhite&blue raised dots
i don't recognize
Enterprise, AL 1968
easter dress, grandma's
yellow flowers on white
who? else will i loose
busy working, education
stitched flowers
                        last centuries
i see cat-eyed glasses, clear
glass beads in this versatility
called "patchwork"

"quilts are the best sleep," Toni says,
"the best sleep"
Miles
is straddling the Zz in JAZZ
gray background
against milk crates holding
my toy piano, poster, toy piano
folk who don't play

get more out of it than i do
i stare my homesick blues
into the keys▲

➤ *Club House* ➤

> *We die unconsciously*
> *Because possessed by a non-human symbol.*
>   Jean Toomer

Twas a pause in the hip hop
brought we to a hard stop
center of Bohemian's.

Room music clubbed we. Nubby
heads twist locked. Boom bam
boom...not silvery like disco
but in that uniform.

We shop use-ta-be chic. Shop
use-ta-be chic. Black robes east coast,
color robs west. We

talk about a movie,
cayenne summer sweat dream,
political phone machine,
Did you do the left (beep)?

Dance floor ear wop. Old rhyme
mimes subculture.▲

Rodney M. McNeil was born in Jersey City, NJ on September 13, 1966. At the present time he resides in Newark, NJ with his parents, Wilbur J. and Betty L. McNeil.

Some of Rodney's first experiences as a writer came under the tutelage of Amiri Baraka at his Malcolm X Writer's Workshop in 1980-81. Rodney wrote his first poem in September 1982 and published "Mirrors in the Room" in 1987, in the journal *Obsidian II*. His poem, "The Radio" was published that same year and he has had work published twice in the *City Sun* (a Brooklyn-based newspaper).

Overall, Rodney hopes to publish his first volume of poetry, *Mirrors: Poems 1984-1988*, and a sequel titled *Sun Dreams*, which will include essays.

Rodney states his educational background has included study at both Hampton and Rutgers (Newark) Universities, where he majored in English.

At the present time he is a hospital clerk at University of Medicine and Dentistry of New Jersey (Newark). He hopes to resume his college studies soon.

"Art is the Body of imagination, and is the cultivation of Hope." ▲

➤*Mirrors In The Room*➤

a poet hung himself today

        a black poet.

        everytime he sat down to put his pen
        to paper it was magic.

        a potential lover said: "you're too
        open-hearted, Art."

        his love was a flowing blue, like a
        river of the mind

and he hung himself, slumped over
black man
——in
        reality

he listened to the rasta's chant
on the slow summer evening

"I don't want to wait in vain, for your love."
is all the long braided African said

    (words flowed from the pen in cursive)

——that sad wanting in his heart

        wanting for love
                for peace
                for welfare
                for
                  a
                    woman
                  and a child
              and the
                whole world to unite on top

together on a bright dawn's day

could not be
answered.

and so he took his brown skin (orange soul)
into a room with some mirrors (the only place he could
get some of himself back)
and

stopped.▲

➤ *An Angel in the Temple of Luxor* ➤

Africa cannot be wounded.
 Her people will not die.
We cannot
 suffer
 the bloody
 pale faces
  around us like "Omega Man."
Egypt, our mighty victory of choice
          will
          last.
the sweet songs of Song–hay !
     the elaborate ornaments of Benin
     the distinguished statutes of Ashanti
     the great people of Bantu
     the love of our one God
         will
          be in
    space and
        time to
     give our lives purpose
       and dignity
       forever
like the Sphinx I sit here.
dry -lipped in the desert but
     brooding
   rain
   inside
       the spirits
   of the blackest
like the Sphinx I stand in anticipation
anticipating my people's explosion
 like an angry rasta's bursting forth
 from a gray basement of tormentors...
our people do shine.
    we must shine.
for all we are worth,
    in God's sight

we shine as his
beloved children.▲

➤*It Just Doesn't Matter*➤

as I lay here alone
        I think of the rejections of hands
                the warm hands reaching out to my
cooling body.
I suddenly turn into a stone man when you
                get close
        the bitterness deep in me breeds bitterness in the rest
        that the melodrama, the tragedy of my little life
        my little world
                little dreams
        has produced the me you see today.
        But we have little minds and can not be humble
        the world is small to those who think they have
        conquered it
            it is enormous, gigantic, we are puny to those
        of us who are the slaves of LIFE and exist
                        continually
                                through
                                        misery.
        If only my mind was expansive enough to contain the
expanse of reality, I would be humble
                                        history.

        I would be humble
                evolution of millions of years on earth
                and
                trillions of years of destruction, crumbling of asteroids
                planets blown up
                ancient egyptian soldiers killed in war
                even world war I
                the small little dreams of an african in the quiet
                rain jungle who
                        fount a stream of
                                water
        as expansive as even this country is
                the world is the earth Planets
                The Milky Way is
                        the Universe is
        and one man carries the burden of it all in his heart

on his mind?
how
dumb and backward can we be
to
   feel the ton ton(s) of the planet Jupiter
   we get depressed, we sometimes, a lot of times
get melancholy
      cause we think we are
            NOTHING
                        (or close to nothing anyway)
but the dark brown Egyptian soldiers died on the sand
the Italians died in tragedy in the 17th century A.D.
            WE ARE PUNY
and that one day my slight melancholy, lucidity and smug
humbleness will not exist
            my body will disintegrate into gas ghostlike gas
            and my memories
               my memory the emotion from the experience
            of the world
                  will not exist
                  I will be a gas unable to THINK
               DO YOU HEAR ME
            we will all be a gas mixing with each other
               like slithering snakes
            yet we will not even be slithering snakes
                  we will be a gas unable to think, unable to feel
            yet we can live
                        today
We can live, dance briefly
      get into joy
and one day our descendents highly evolved amphibious
water people will pity and have deep compassion for us
the souls in us, that we are locked in these primitive
brains, and say damn with a drop of a tear
      and look upon this as a dark period
               that the spirits in us our greater than us
                  than WE ARE
even my rejection of nice girls
      and the guilt that I must feel
         underneath

will not exist
the age of "immortal men" should be destructed
        there are no "immortal men"
        and I'm not just saying that because I'm not
        a legend
                I'm not a myth or I'm not great or something or
                another
        nothing that is alive in this transient form changing
        world exists in the same shape it is in now-forever
                        even "Rock" Hudson changed
        even Muhammad Ali changed
                        and you
                                named your son after him
        down with the myth of the
                        small stagnant office world that you
                        think isn't past the Bahamas
        down with you conquering the world in your sleep
        down with me conquering the world in my sleep
                if we could stretch our minds
                                        to
                                        know

        the vastness of the universe,
                history, time
                in history
        changing matter, dying people
                        little thoughts
                        the little dream in
        your head
                the small fear in your soul
                the slight depression in your
                mind
                will last and be remembered
        as much as
                the egyptian warrior who died
                        9,463 years
                                ago
                                        in
                                        the
                                        sand. ▲

Tony Medina, Puerto Rican poet, born on January 10, 1966 in the South Bronx, NY. Grew up in the Bronx, attended P.S. 72, J.H.S. 101, graduated from Norman Thomas H.S. Did a three-year bid in the white man's army to earn money for college, was married, now divorced and attending apartheid-like Baruch College, where he had been booted out a semester and went back, only to be banned from the school paper. But has started, along with activist professors & students, an alternative newsletter aimed at exposing the backward reactionary racist dog administration & fight for a curriculum of inclusion. Tony's first volume of poetry, *Emerge & See*, was published in 1991. Currently living in Harlem, U.S.A., Medina is also at work on various cultural-political-literary projects, including his second book of poetry.▲

➤ *rhudine rhudine* ➤

rhudine rhudine
i saw you shuffling
in your half-trod
down beaten walk
cradling a bottle
of beer beneath
a bloated arm
rhudine
who did not love you
back in the days
when you used to be
laid out on street corners
and in alleyways
in your half-drunk
blackout blues
who kicked you out
when you were only
thirteen
and who filled you
full of heroin and
sperm, sent you hurling
in your nappy head
despair calling you
ugly, kicking you
in your gut, spattin
your face
rhudine
i saw you shuffling
in your half-trod
down beaten walk
in your plaid shirt
and burgundy cuffs
scraping beneath
your swollen shoes,
you turned to smile
and your huge brown
pupils drowned

in a yellow sea
of pain, rhudine
or was that the
blues singing in
your eyes or was
that the blues
singing in your
eyes or was that
the blues singing
when i saw you shuffling
back to the homeless shelter▲

➤ don't say goodnight
to etheridge knight ➤

59
and the
cancer creeped
your lung, heavy
mucous lead
wrapped its
tentacles around
your bloated vein
less neck, your
heart collapsed
the music in you,
your final broken
air taking flight
among the birds &
the angels of the night.
don't say goodnight
to etheridge knight
his body freed from
sight, his blue black
music mingling in the
heart and ear of the night,
a radar poet black voodoo
priest with the pain
and fear of a nation boiling
on a twisted cooker boiling
in a boiling spoon boiling
through a broke tip boiling
needle boiling through a vein
less arm of sweet empty gut
hollow pit of eyes and crushed
nut rage boiling to a boiling
point of infinite volcanic eruptions
of self destructive vomit clutching
the guts and burning nuts like lead
cobwebs dragging and drying the insides

of dead pink flesh and shrinking eye jones.
don't say goodnight
to etheridge knight
whose soul ate shrapnel
in a korean field
who did an 8 year bid
in the white man's can
who said he couldn't
but could and did and wrote
and sang and dug the word
and dug sonia and dug trane
and bird and gwendolyn brooks
and sterling brown dug the jive
and the juju and the boogaloo
dug the funky bebop rhythm
of a harlem street walker
caked in blues payin the
white man's dues like
jesus carrying some wood
on his back like billie
stretched out on a nightclub
rack blue black blue black
blue black purple and bruised
don't say goodnight
to the music of the man
who sang of shine
who sang of red malcolm
love and rage who sang
of the sweet smiling dancing
eyes of children
who sang of life and
beauty and prison and
scag and wine
don't say goodnight
to etheridge knight
up in heaven playin
bebop and salsa
with miguel pinero
lucky cienfuegos

and larry neal
with sweet sassy sarah
and dexter gordon
don't say goodnight
to etheridge
his parting may bring the night
but the memory of his music
will bring back the mornin▲

➤ *Poem For Teacup Mantlepiece Poets Palpitating Poot Booty Plagiarists Imprisoned In Ivy League White Supremacist Mental Biological Warfare Labs*➤

Do the people
like it motherfucker
Do the people
like it motherfucker
Do the people
like it motherfucker
motherfuckers writing that
teacup mantlepiece shit,
reading poetry by the fire,
curled by a fireplace
while the poor oppressed
masses stay out in the
snow & cold in tents,
hungry & screaming
for their heads!
a teacup on the mantlepiece
of white supremacy
Ivy league
constipated
pedantic dribble
drabble hard
doe doe for
birds
sitting on
electrocuted
nest eggs.
do the people
like it motherfucker
do the people
like it motherfucker
juxtaposing this,
enjambing that
shoving a goddamn motherfuckin
adjective here & there.

all that library
shit, all
that high art
mantlepiece shit
that motherfuckers can't reach
'cause they too poor to shine the door
knobs of supremacist mansions
& libraries w/they
rusty crusty calloused
hands
do the people understand it motherfucker
do the people understand it,
get your confused asses
out of Harvard &
Yale
Come back to 135th & Lenox
Come back to Huntspoint
& Southern Blvd,
Come back to Watts &
Newark
Come back to Kingston &
Puerto Rico,
to the people
Come back to
the motherfuckin
people come back
to the beautiful
loving people come
back to the people
that gave birth to
you come back to
the people that
gave you attitude,
come back to pistol whippings
& block parties,
come back to nickle bags
hidden in socks & running
down alleys, come back
to grassroots reality

come back to congas
& boogaloo come back to
brown wild-haired double-dutch
jumpin mommies & tamarindo taino
salsa merenge blues people
comeback to pidagua carts &
puerto rican rum & gin on
a harlem stoop, come back
to ray baretto prraakkating ting ting
tito puente on percussion, bird & trane on sax
pistol whipping bill collectors
with mesmerizing muscatel madness
come back to the people come back
to the people let the people come back
to the people let the people under
stand your shit let the poeple
dig your shit love the people
& the people will love you
be a lover of the people
be a lover of the people
be a lover of the people
& not a lonely pouting motherfucker
masturbating in a corner
be a hot jalapeño
acapurria chitterlin gumbo
collard green black bean
soy bean
pig gut
pig feet
rot gut blues
singer assaulting vultures
w/your breath & tongue,
be a lover
be a lover
be a lover
yeah.▲

David S. Mills: Born in Brooklyn, NY on October 10, 1965.
M.A. (creative writing) New York University, 1990.
B.A. Yale University, 1988.
Teaches poetry and playwriting in schools, battered women shelters and prisons. I have a cut (entitled "Ghost Town") released on Steve Coleman's new album *Black Science.* I've done voice-overs for radio. I've also done freelance writing for *Essence, Emerge, The Village Voice, The City Sun,* and *Crisis Magazine.*▲

➤ *Chembank Card* ➤

I insert the blue and silver
Card in the cash machine
Ultraviolet LED readout:
"Withdraw, balance inquiry,
Deposit, transfer." I select withdraw
Amount must be divisible by $10
I press 3; I press 0
In the 52 seconds it takes
For my green to come out
The money's ink is mingled
With the crimson blood
Of a Sowetan in a double-talk
Holding cell. Legs and feet
Bound to two tables:
He swings like a leather hammock
Welts rise up on his back
Like leavened dough.
Official report: Suicide
By hanging. The people's report:
He was killed
For not committing treason
Against his own reason.
My cash is ready. It's regurgitated
From a mechanical mouth
Along with my balance.   (pull $)
The machine finally lights up,
"Would you like another transaction?"
The selections:
"Yes or No."
I'd like to press never. ▲

➤And Now Yu➤

*I'm begging on my knees please wait. I don't even know who your girlfriend
is. I just came here to look at a car. No! You was fucking my girlfriend!*
Yusef and Fama's exchange
If Keith goes to jail he'll be in there with all those blacks.
Angela, Keith Mondello's ex.

Ink ain't spewed from this pen
Like the sangria from your guinea riddle heart.
Aryan approximations Mondellos, Rauccis
Carreris, Patinos and Famas claimed a corner
Of the city unsuitable for black car buyers.
Yu was gang banged
Over the confused turf most white men get
Pigs eyes over, pink pussy, notably Gina Feliciano:
She ruined the neighborhood.

Last Saturday and Tuesday's humid exchange
About thick African vines twisting
Through the heart of Gina's white darkness
Turned into Wednesday night's melee and murder.
Gina refused Fama
A hole for his puppy jism
So he pumped his load into Yu
Sef
Spent.

The News

No one cried wolfpack;
The killers were not called animals;
Trump didn't take out any hate ads;
And Morton Downey forgot to call them
Bastards: The motive was only skin deep.

III

John Gotti's the darling of Bensonhurst
Where Guidos cruise chics in souped up cars
And Italian men play cards on folding tables

While their wives chat in front of the seductive
Smells of the bakery's fresh cannoli.
Saturday they brandished watermelons
Like pistols and hurled insults
At the mirror of their fears:

"Der makin' a big deal out of dis. I'd a slapped
Her myself if she was wid a black guy. I wouldn't
Let her degrade herself like dat. Blacks should know
Not to visit Bensonhurst at night. Dese streets are safe
To walk at night. If dey come back
Dey'll get more of da same."

IV
The trigger man's admired uncle was busted
with 3 mil' in stash and 7 mil' in heroin
On his 51st birthday Surprise!
Most of that was aimed at the Bedstuys:
The unsolved murders.

V
Uncle Ben who hires whites
To execute his own
in the name of blue suits and sirens
Said "It's an aberration. This is
The kind of community that makes the city
Work."

His hinchmen silenced
Eleanor Bumpers
Michael Stewart
Oliver James Williams
Richard Luke
Alfred Sanders
Yvonne Smallwood
Nicholas Bartlett
Kevin Thorpe

Their relatives attacked

Fabrice Thebaud
Charles Hohn
Raymond Buckner
Sylvester Lamont
Steven Lamont
Artes Williams
Samuel Spencer dead
Michael Griffith dead
Willie Turks dead
And Now Yu
Sef
Dead!▲

Gavin Moses grew up in Ardmore, PA. He moved to New York City, where he earned degrees from New York University and the Columbia University Graduate School of Journalism. His poems have appeared in such publications as *Quatro*, *Icarus* and *Long Shot*, and will be featured as one of four poets in *New New York* (Nuyorican Press). Gavin got his poetic push in 1979 at the Nuyorican Poets Cafe when playwright Miguel Piñero told him to "read another one." Since then Gavin has been active in New York's new cafe poetry scene reading his works at colleges, festivals and such places as the Nuyorican Poets Cafe, ABC No Rio, The Knitting Factory and St. Marks Poetry Project. Gavin is founding member of Poets 4, a multi-generational jazz-blues poetry collective and was a finalist in the Poets Cafe Grand Slam, as well as a member of the New York team of the National Poetry Slam (1991). He is employed as a reporter at *People* magazine.▲

➤ *A Poem for Trish* ➤

Word iz
in Greenwich Village
on 6th ave. & w. 4th st.
Trish sells Malcolm X posters
by
any-means-necessary
for $3.00
in between stalking buyers
her eyes
dance furiously about with
motions & e-motions
she mixes metaphors while effervescent
smiles leap out of her mouth
aiding her poli-sci-co-logically
black mind-set on "the" revolution &
life before the Atlantic crossing
her arms
wave-point-shake-out at
people who she knows, know not who they are
& they take from her a smile & a lesson
the only white that she cares to touch
lies around the border of a poster that
frames Malcolm
his profile bleeds against its snowy
backdrop
both he & she won't
surrender
because something iz at stake

Trish sells move-ment posters
in Greenwich Village
Africa dangles from her ears
Word iz
Trish iz pushin' a legend
by any-means-necessary. ▲

➤ *Black Banana House* ➤

Bony, pubescent, boys body pulled
rubber-band-back, chicken wing-like
42nd St. cop to punk control brace.
Then locked in master bedroom closet,
a screaming human hamper. Sprained spring
spirit confused.

Mom not home. Husband, stepfather, yanked fuses,
threw phobic food fits. Always, always drank
first. Wuz last lamenting drunk leaving Bailey's
brawling bar. At home: unwinding chanting
bitch, whore, football fearing faggot names.

Beneath the pale peel of brightness
I am a prisoner at Auschwitz hungry for God.
I am Mandela remembering the sun.

Before dawn, droning adolescent bodies rise to
wedge grown up bodies slam-thumping bedroom
walls. Fear shackles words hanging still
like sconces. Sister's face punched by familiar
hands fingering up pulled covers for honeysuckle
sweetness. Had we banana skin the world would
have seen the spiraling blotches that blackened
our slender souls. ▲

Willie Perdomo is a writer living in East Harlem. He is the winner of the 1990 Nuyorican Poets Cafe Grand Slam. His work has recently appeared in PBS's *Alive From Off Center* Series entitled "Words in Your Face," and he participated in the 1991 National Poetry Slam in Chicago. He has read at major universities and colleges in the Tri-State area and his work will appear in an anthology *New New York*. He has completed his first book, *Where a Nickel Costs a Dime.* ▲

➤ *Unemployed Mami* ➤

Even though she don't have a job, mami still works
hard. The last twenty-three years of her life have been
spent teaching a poet and killing generations of cock-
roaches with sky-blue plastic slippers, t.v. guides, and
pink tissues. She prays for the poet as he runs into the
street looking for images of Boricua sweetness to explode
in his face. The young roaches escape in the dark while
my unemployed mami goes to sleep cursing at them.

Even though she don't have a job, mami still works
hard. She walked behind my drunken father, in the rain,
as he stumbled into manhood and oblivion in America,
wearing his phony mambo elegance of pinky rings and
processed hair. He beat my mami, he beat my mami, stop
beating my mami with the black umbrella; the one with
the fake ivory horsehead handle. I still hear the same
salsa coming out the same social club where I use to
fall asleep and dream about a happy life.

Even though she don't have a job, mami still works
hard. Every year she prays for abuela who died in a sweet
bed of Holy Water y Ben Gay while the poet was kicking his
mother inside her stomach. Mami looks at Miss America,
Miss Universe, Miss Everything, every year and then she
runs into her bedroom to dig out her highschool yearbook
from underneath the pile of important papers. "Look, Papo.
Look at me when I was a teenager. I was pretty like those
girls on t.v." You still are, I say to my sacred mami
Carmen.

Even though she don't have a job, mami still works
hard. Lately, she plays slow songs of lost love over and
over and over. She looks out the window only when it
rains, measuring the tear drops against the rain drops.
    Where is that man? I wonder as I sit in my room writing
and rewriting this poem for her. I catch her peeking at
me from the corner of her eye, wondering if I do, *I really*

do, love you and that's not the record, that's me, I say
hugging her.

Don't cry, mami.

Even though you don't have a job, I know you still be
working hard.▲

➤ *Revolutionary* ➤

The most
revolutionary act
I've ever seen
was the night
Crazy Cano
told officer Rooney

> *Muthafucka*
> *Take off your badge*
> *and gun*
> *and see if*
> *I don't bust*
> *your ass*
> *all the way back*
> *to the precinct*

That was
the most
revolutionary act
I have ever
seen▲

➤ *Nigger-Reecan Blues* ➤
(for Piri Thomas)

Hey, Willie. What are you, man? Boricua? Moreno? Que?

I am.

No, silly. You know what I mean: What are you?

I am you. You are me. We the same. Can't you feel our veins
drinking the same blood?

> -But who said you was a Porta Reecan?
> -Tu no ere Puerto Riqueno, brother.
> -Maybe Indian like Ghandi Indian.
> -I thought you was a Black man.
> -Is one of your parents white?
> -You sure you ain't a mix of something like
> -Portuguese and Chinese?
> -Naaaahhhh...You ain't no Porta Reecan.
> -I keep telling you: The boy is a Black man with an accent.

If you look closely you will see that your spirits are standing
right next to our songs. Yo soy Boricua! Yo soy Africano! I
ain't lyin'. Pero mi pelo es kinky y kurly y mi skin no es negro
pero it can pass...

> -Hey, yo. I don't care *what* you say—you Black.

I ain't Black! Everytime I go downtown la madam blankeeta de
madeeson avenue sees that I'm standing right next to her and
she holds her purse just a bit tighter. I can't even catch a
taxi late at night and the newspapers say that if I'm not in
front of a gun, chances are that I'll be behind one. I wonder why...

> -Cuz you Black, nigger.

I ain't Black, man. I had a conversation with my professor. Went
like this:

-Where are you from, Willie?
-I'm from Harlem.
-Ohh! Are you Black?
-No, but—
-Do you play much basketball?

- Te lo estoy diciendo, brother. Ese hombre es un moreno!
Miralo!

Mira yo no soy moreno! I just come out of Jerry's Den and the coconut
spray off my new shape-up sails around the corner, up to the Harlem
River and off to New Jersey. I'm lookin' slim and I'm lookin' trim
and when my homeboy Davi saw me, he said: "Coño, Papo. Te parece como
un moreno, brother. Word up, bro. You look like a stone black
kid."

- I told you-you was Black.

Damn! I ain't even Black and here I am sufferin' from the young
Black man's plight/the old white man's burden/and I ain't even
Black, man/A Black man/I am not/Boricua I am/ain't never really
was/Black/like me...

-Leave that boy alone. He got the Nigger-Reecan Blues

I'm a Spic!
I'm a Nigger!
Spic! Spic! No different than a Nigger!
Neglected, rejected, oppressed and depressed
From banana boats to tenements
Street gangs to regiments...
Spic! Spic! I ain't nooooo different than a Nigger.▲

Kevin Powell, 26, was born in Jersey City, NJ. and studied at Rutgers University. Now a resident of New York City, Kevin is a freelance journalist whose articles, essays, and reviews have appeared in *Essence, Vibe, The New York Times, Rolling Stone, Emerge, The Source,* and *L.A. Weekly.* Kevin is a contributor to *Brotherman* (Random House), the forthcoming anthology of Black men writers edited by Herb Boyd and Robert Allen. Kevin is also featured on MTV's "The Real World," a documentary which explores the lives of seven young people living together in a New York City. An award-winning poet, Kevin has read his poetry and lectured at several universities and colleges throughout the nation and has been published in various magazines and journals. He is co-editor of the *Young Tongues* anthology series of chapbooks featuring up-and-coming Black writers and a contributing editor to *Eyeball,* a new multicutural literary journal. Kevin's first volume of poetry, *don't feel no way,* is forthcoming from First Civilizations, Inc. and he is at work on a novel, *diary of a b-boy.* ▲

➤*for aunt cathy*➤

life ain't never been promised to nobody
that's what grandma lottie used to say
and you
her youngest daughter
and youngest of six children
snuck into the city
on a greyhound bus
with my mother
and scraped the side of a boarding house for good luck
as your life stretched beyond
the wooden shacks
and cotton fields
and the sandy school room floors of south carolina

and you were alive
at last
free
in a city
away from the
comforting stench of down south
and in the big city
with its
musty underarm
and gasoline breath

and you took all ten years of your schoolin'
and applied for a job as a factory worker
on the assembly line
and you assembled parts
and the parts assembled you into
the permanence of minimum wages
and timeclocks
and bosses who thought a black woman
was supposed to like work
hell, y'all had been conditioned to be oxes
they figured

and when you wasn't producing like an ox
their tucked-in pot bellies would ask:
why you moving so slow cathy?
and on the inside you licked your tongue
at them the way you used to do
when my mother and aunt birdie yelled at you
and your heart tightened around your waist
and you ate what your feet could produce
for eight hours a day
40 hours a week
with
one 15 minute break a day
if you was doing your job

and you needed something else
to keep your tears from spitting out
thoughts and words that would send you
back down south
in a fit of fear
and you met him
and he was fine
that man
and you liked him
and he liked you
and like became love
to you
and like became lust
for him
and he and you
exploded into anthony
my cousin anthony
one april day in 1966
and now you had a shield
to hold against the world
you had a world to shield you against
the heartaches of him
the footaches of work
and the headaches
of city life

and you raised anthony
the best way you knew how
just like my mother raised me
and anthony grew and i grew
with our frustrated imaginations
to resent each other
to hate you, our mothers
to despise our very existences
in that tiny
cramped three-room apartment
two mothers and two sons
in a three-room apartment
held together
by welfare
foodstamps
and the roaches
who always found their way
into our food
no matter how thick
the layers of aluminum foil

and that thirsty, tingling sensation
would often reappear
crawling between your toes
up your legs
across your thighs
teasing your crotch
but it couldn't get any further
that's nasty,
you thought,
some man between my legs
again
so you stuffed your womb
with the world of anthony
because your spirit
was tired of being probed
by social workers, mailmen, and would-be husbands
for having an illegitimate son

and in spite of reality
burning down every hope we had
we managed to spread out
to a better part of the ghetto
and we even had separate apartments now
but you and my mother
always was in the same building because
my mother was the mean one
who scoffed at the world
with her angry eyes
and you was the nice one
who wanted to be like my mother
but you couldn't
so you followed my mother
everywhere
because at least you'd be safe
from yourself

and when we finally moved out of the ghetto
around white folks
you felt good
we was movin' up
and flying like birds released
from their mother's grip for the first time
and we was happy to be around
white folks
and didn't mind being called niggas
because at least we was good niggas

and me and anthony
knocked off the weight of
that restless city
that dirty city
and we left:
me to college
anthony to the navy
leaving you and my mother
grazing in the pastures of mid-life

and my mother was happy to be free of a man-child
but you was sad
because anthony had been your reason to live
your reason to work
your reason to exist
and now his departure meant your death
and you were dying
a slow death
dancing with mid-life and dying a muted death
the years of working were gone
the years of sharing were gone
the years of being were gone
and the woman inside of your crouching body
died one may day in 1988 when grandma lottie was buried
and as we wiped the tears from our eyes
no one noticed you sinking through the church pew
through the floor
into the earth to join grandma lottie

and even though anthony was there at the funeral
he left again
back to the navy
back to japan
to some strange place
that was not him
because he hated himself
and he hated you
for being him
and he nailed shut
the door
on your life

and no one noticed you drowning in your pain
until you began having conversations with yourself
and tellin' everyone how you was hearing things
and seeing movies on your living room wall
how you was the star in those movies

and even my mother

with her superstitious ways
could not believe
that you were a victim of roots and magic spells

and my mother and aunt birdie did it;
they tricked you with a meal and had you straitjacketed
and they didn't tell me
but i found out and i found you
and i leaped inside your body
and begged you to wake up
i swam inside your dried up tears
and turned back the currents
to your childhood
to your adolescence
to your early adulthood
to anthony
to anthony's father
to my mother and aunt birdie and grandma lottie
and i cried between the lines of your history

and you told me you were not crazy
and i said i know
and you told me you could not understand
why my mother and aunt birdie had put you there
and i said i know
and you told me how they drugged you
how they called you by a number
how they monitored your phone calls
and i new that you had become a prisoner of your worst fears
of your own death

and i looked at you and i didn't see you
instead i saw an old black woman
inside your 45-year-old body
and i wanted to rush to you and shake your youth
out of that imposter

but it was you...

and now i understand those sounds you heard
and those movies you saw on your walls
you are not crazy
it took me a long time
but i understand
anthony knows what you've been through
but he doesn't know you
i know you
my mother and aunt birdie know what you've been through
but they don't know you
i know you

i carry you with me everyday
i see you when i see that black woman
lying on the ground with a mcdonald's cup in her hand
at 34th street
i see you and i say
"here cathy,
this is all i got"
and i drop a tear into your cup
and curse myself and my mother and aunt birdie
and anthony and anthony's father
and i kiss you with a prayer
because now i understand
why black bodies sag the way they do
and why black hearts don't birth emotions anymore▲

---

[1] *yebo* means "yes" in the Zulu language (indigenous to South Africa)

➤*love/a many splintered thing*➤
for Karla

i have this need to feel you
make love out of the sweat
itching our palms give
you to your mother so that she
can give birth to you create an
ocean where love sleeps peacefully
eat out of the same bed we flesh
orgasms scream where cobwebs
imprison courage cry where
your tears gripped my shoulders wrap
my tongue around your waist and
lick the rhythms of your walk
talk until a beat hits me where
it hits me where it hits me
in the space   where my heart
used to be   you know it's
blank now dark black no
commercials open land
waiting to be folded and smoothed
out like the note i slipped you yesterday
that said you are me am you we are
do not be afraid i want to
help you help me love a
many splintered thing i felt
yes his tongue slit my heart
as it parted your mouth
and i wanted to die yeah
rope myself with my naivete
drink reflection: share a walk on
lenox avenue with a friend who
gets high on pain too many times
we step on our eyelids and miss
the chance to l(i)ove the chance
to slide open a cloud with a kiss
when will trust not be for sale a
gun between the thighs a middle

finger aimed at the hungry a wish
stuffed inside two bodies crawling
on their tails scraping the bottom
of a dream▲

➤*Mental Terrorism*➤

i wonder what wright and baldwin
        and all the other soothsayers
would say
if they could witness
the after effects
of the calculated explosion
        of 5 billion inhuman minds?

funny
        how things
                have gotten to this

vacant hearts have taken each other hostage
        and stumble forward
heading no where in particular
        doing nothing in particular
                looking for mr. or ms. goodbar

the hero of the day:
        nelson mandela
yebo![1]
let's name a candy bar after him
        name it the freedom bar
rich
chocolate-
flavored
crunch
        that chips a tooth on every second byte
and if someone fucks with you or me
        it converts into a semi-automatic ninja fighter
complete with copies of "the art of war,"
"the anarchist cookbook,"
and the holy bible

(of course
        if you forget to freeze the bar
                it will be quite ineffective as a means of deterrence)

nel son man de la
will you free me please?
        i've never met god
but
you sure are close
we love you mr. mandela
        what is love anyway?
my mother and i
have never hugged
        have never kissed
            have never said
"i love you"
call me a stupefied stoic
        however
the world's bloody palms
have yet to clutch my face
        in pity

what is it to be locked away
        in the imagination of kidnappers—
an unwanted and unappreciated spoil of war?

"underdog!
oh where oh where can my underdog be?"
bart simpson and arsenio hall
        in that order
are the only two friends i have left
they will soon become bigger
        than all the gods
in ancient africa
and forget that humankind exists day to day

can i cry in living color?
from buckwheat to the homeboy shopping network
        will the negro ever learn the concept
of self-respect?
edutainment is the key
        flip a switch
and rap a lyric

        around a little kid's brain
call it
video music box
      and yo! mtv raps
the music of rebellious generation
           generating truth from beneath the rubbish
of integrated nightmares

rhyth mic american po e try
      you hear it
         and you think of me
trapped in a concrete box
         begging to be released
so that i can be told a thousand and one times
"well, you have a nice resume but..."
how many buts can one man have anyway?
      and some of you have the nerve to condemn the homeless!
all i want is the opportunity to have an opportunity
      where does one run to when *stuck* in the promised land?
how about central park?
      the beast is smilin'
      'cuz he went wildin'
in the dark
(Black folks never heard of the word "wildin" until 1989)
        total recall is only a movie
      coerced confessions
are revisited from scottsboro

              (central park, too, deserves a song)

the sperm don't match
      hoover's boys said that
i guess
somebody's gotta pay
      for purity's guilt

only if malcolm had lived
      only if martin had lived
         only if the dead kennedys would rise

one eye on the prize
        the other on the bush-man
flip-flopping like a misplaced fish on the beach
                creating political vision
                        without political backbone

don't touch that flag!
        it's live campaign ammunition

N-E-A stands for
Nazism Entering America
via congressional doors
2   bad   and   2   live
                for the average citizen who hasn't read machiavelli
        or tricky dicky nixon's lips

censoring is moral mccarthyism
        and the 90's version of the lynch mob

                                big bother is watching you
        watching me

i can't stop writing
                in spite of my fears
who cares?

it's gettin'
        it's gettin'
                it's gettin' kinda hectic
but i've got the power to break out of this cage at any moment...▲

➤*Southern Birth*➤

(for Lottie Burrison Powell, February 23, 1912-May 16, 1988)

a procession. southern wails. a yellow
face emerges specked with black moles.
two pennies slit the eyes where the dirt road
used to be. those thick glasses
distract from the tobacco-stained
teeth. tingling carolina stench braid
coarse charcoal hair.

i ache until it is wet, naked,
full of bounce: a gushing wind
corners a heart; puffy cotton veins
snap the way grandma lottie
broke string beans in the front yard.
a moist sound spills onto
the dirty plywood. reverend wilson's
eulogy fogs the church. homemade
syrup and cornbread descend. my mouth
plummets into an emotional abyss: a lover
flees the outhouse and a baby inherits the pain.▲

➤*don't feel no way*➤
(for South-Central L.A. & "The Real World" fanatics)

yo bust it: a lost generation
creeps on its telegenic toes
making the best of all possible worlds
out of no world at all all the world
is a staged coup
a beam-me-up-scotty-double-dutch
with tarot cards flipped by a hip hopper
named heather b.
i don't care 'cuz none of y'all can beat me
peep this homey: that may be true but who can
you beat to set your record straight
crazy horse & hardcore hip hop will surely die
as long as we got m.c. serch in search
of stiff black thighs and sweet potato pie

but yo dig, my man norman said he was
not black or white gay or straight
human or alien
kevin, why do you have to categorize everything?
i come to everyone blank
and, kevin, i do think you have a pattern of aggressive
behavior; you're always pushing me into a corner
yes, i'm neutral kevin, you know, like my big picture

dig if you will a picture
of me and innocent julie engaged in a dish—
inner-city blues and southern-fried
hospitality to go
naive american princess (nap) you dis me
you cry the venom that drips from
my african beads don't tell me that you
understand 'til you hear this man
youknowhatahmsayin', hear? hair?
right here? right here lawd right here?!?
mtv ain't down with the naugh-ty
by nature

ghetto bastards we are
more than a twisted sisterbrother rippin'
lyrics and lives insideupsidedown
from compton to da boogie down
my development been arrested by all
the flyboys (like eric) with buttermilk skin

do he always gotta talk about that skin thing man?
he's bitter that's why
goddamn right i'm bitter
it's better than being butter
spread like clarence thomas
across america's ass cheeks

i speak we speak new speak
the language of a hip hop nation
the niggerati literati:
greg tate joan morgan scott poulson-bryant dream hampton
danyel smith bonz malone james bernard
offering an anti-colonial salvation
d-d-d-don't be afraid
we won't hurt you our name is not
columbus and we don't have any
cheap trinkets to bribe you with

but i don't feel no way   andre's hair (you hear?)
side-swipes bemusedly
well ain't that some shit?
andre is the most relaxed motherfucka
this side of a graveyard
(least he admits he has a pop martyr complex)

smells like a mean spirit
reigning and dancing on my grill
knuckle up!
and choose your weapon g
1 motherfuckin' 2 motherfuckin' eye & i wanna be free...

i once had expectations of da m 2 da e 2 da u

but the 90s is here, yeah, i taste it
everytime i hear bullets punch a hole in harlem's heart
or watch integrated lovers in the village
ask me for approval with their
tarzan-meets-shaniqua guilt complexes

momma never said there would be days like
these but she did say if you make yo' bed
hard you sleep in it hard
given my basic instincts i can't have a hard-on
for too long   it causes the eight ball to flip pool games
over and even the score a little ain't that how the
panel of gods planned it danielle?

p-p-please kill the daisies becky!
yeah, america is a young country but who said
you had to be old to be a tyrant, ya dig?
i just reached birthday #26 and every night
before i lay my head down to sleep i thank
the gods for loaning me another day
that feminist/environmental bullshit don't mean
nothin' to a nigga who picks roaches out of
his spaghetti every night

and now for a cnn newsbreak(north!)—
u-uh they don't stop
whippin' the love off
sweaty black souls
(if we just angle correctly,
we can get the nigga's whole body into the oven mr. president)
the daisy age is over
slavery's not back in effect
it never left
just been civil right-ed and we are the world-ed
a deep cover for a nightmare comin'
to a major city near you

we are goin' out big time and no one realizes it
front page news:

all i know (#69) is
a nigga toad was found guilty of
being justifiably beaten
by racist 5-O
said freeze!
and they pissed on brotha rodney
can he really tell them he never had a gun?
it's the black asses that's gettin' done
turn el-ay turn i smell a riot
goin' on yeah sure right we'll control
our frustrations
but it'll take a blacknation
40 acres and a mule
to the millionth power to do it

have you ever visited a country that eats its young
then pits them against each other like animals?
(hell, if the cops would have beaten a dog from beverly hills
they would have been found guilty on all counts)
but now we have a lootin' spree
(when did they stop countin' us as three-fifths of a human target?)
the looters are comin' the looters are comin'
(starring ice cube and ice-t)
keep the niggas in south-central
while the bush-man and wild bill jockey for
position in the race to race the race against the race

don't feel no way y'all
da boyz n the hood will right a poetic justice
& my homeys john singleton & tupac know what time it is
the loft the loft the loft is on fire this time
and ain't no water left to put
out the future...▲

Linwood M. Ross was born January 18, 1959, in Rice, VA. He barely escaped the remnants of jim crowism when his family booked to the uptown-plantation-zoo's of New York. Graduated from F.I.T. with a degree in communications. He currently works as a sales representative and freelance columnist to afford the spiritual luxury of being an artist.

Currently residing (surviving) in Port Chester, NY. his work has appeared in *Aim, Black American Literature Forum, Catalyst, Changing Men, Essence, Free Lunch, Felicity, Haight Ashbury Literary Journal, Impetus, Lactuca, The Moment, Notebook, Poetry Forum, Poked with Sticks, San Fernando Poetry Journal, Struggle, Word & Image* and others. Winner of 1991 Pushcart Prize for Poetry.

His play "God, I Want Diana Ross' Life" (no relation) has been performed on stage. He is working on his third play and his first collection of poetry.

POETIC GOAL: To record the black-out-loud truth of an African man's experience in America, as he sees, feels, hears, tastes and smells it. ▲

➤*James Brown*➤

Vivid summers of my kidhood were
  lived inside your music, man
    this infectious boogiemusic
     blastin from the "Colored Center's" jukebox
      hot music burnin like wildfire in our legs and feets
     when everybody fell willin and sweatin victims
    to a rapid dance craze, lost inside that sound
    of the amazin "Fabulous Flames"!

And James Brown demanded Maceo to blow
 his horny horn
  & all summer long life became the manic
   rhythm of a driving funk song
    a hardcore, raw bass in yo face
     an anthem
      of black people everywhere
       to be proud of our race
        "say it loud" music comin from all over the place
         the windows & the doorways of the projects
        blastin from the stereo's & the radios
        across inner cities everywhere the music
       blastin...lastin bout 3 maybe 4
      good weeks of jammin
      before the d.j. announces
     we was in for more

And at 13, my ghetto dream was to work
  in a record store
  & i would be hip
  & cool by association
   reveling in the funky notion
    of spinning your records all day
    me, the junior—soul bro
     spreadin the boogieword of
     your new sensation
      "Maaaaaaannnn...have you heard the new James Brown

cut!"

to 1989
  & the bizarre wheels of just-us
    soul brothers
     doin hard time
      & the hardest workin man
       in show business
        watches the slow repetition of days   slide away

And they've silenced the godfather of soul
  a man
   with the explosive genius
    of making a generation dance
     & think
      at the same time.

And lately i've been diggin on the ironic jam:
  "this is a man's world"
   this is a man's world
    but it don't mean nothin..."

in a place where
 it ain't never been no black man's world
  even if he can split, spin & twirl
   even if he can camelwalk
    even if he SCREEEEEEAMS
     falls on his knees
      breaks out in a cold sweat
       & begs: "please please please"

this here   ain't   no black man's world...
  never been
   even if he does possess black magic
    & a soul talent
     for making a spectacle

   of himself. ▲

➤ *Indecent Exposure (A True Story)*➤

Yesterday, I exposed myself on the train.
Maybe, I should say, I FREED my shackled "nigguh"
Sent him sailin thru the stagnant blonde and blue air...
Where the gray flannels & wing-tips sat silently despisin me
& my black   & blue jean essence. Did I care?

Composed &alone squintin at daydreams   & Harlem
In the window. Till I feel their eyes. Ever notice their
Eyes? Somethin happens to them when they rush by this
Community that mirrors ME...Seems like wall street. journals,
The new york times, their harlequin romances & their blinders
Are lowered. As I dig on their haircuts turnin...
& THOSE EYES narrowin in wonder   & pity...
Attracted & repulsed at the sight   Of Harlem.
Shhhhhiiiiiit! Never have they been so grateful to be white,
Then when they glance her abandoned buildings,
Her hoodlums & her Heroes & her Credits & her zeroes
Her scores of inner city lives goin bout the jive business of
Livin. Maaaaaaaaaan... They fall in love all over again
With their whiteness!

As the parade of me...marches in. Anointing the box cars
With my black smell...I am young. I am old. I am weary.
And fatigued. I am traveling alone. I am traveling with
my Kids. I am every color every hue & persuasion invadin
THEIR space. Yo, check out my hi-top fade! Yo, do you DREAD
My locks, baby? Yo, dig my African Lapas cloth head joint!
Yo, dig my $125 sneakers! & my fierce leather, baby! People
have lost their lives for one of these muthafuckas! & dig my
brotha readin Malcolm silently his w/black thoughts Racing,
pounding LOUD as a beat-box, FULL BLAST!

I am not showin my ass, repeat I am NOT showin my ass
Dat way some negroes do. Dat free-style way some like to
Display this fake freedom
Of black man w/ nothin to do...

Some hidin in the bathroom forcin themselves to smell
All their shit...just to get a free-ride...
But I am above that dogshit. I am neither bold or righteous,
Just po enuff to REFUSE to pay. The conductor
Who IS paid large to be on hard nigguhwatch, 24-7...
Ambles up to ME? Demadin MY fare..? SHHHIIITTT!
I tell him, "I paid" ... (In my mind, I am not lyin)
While he's steady replyin" "NO YOU HAVEN'T BOSS!
That'll be $4.75, right now, OR GET THE HELL OFF!

NOW I HAVE to display a little 'tude (like, it's a must!):
"LOOK MAN AIN'T nuthin goin on here! AND I Told you I
PAID!
NOW STEP OFF!" Then I gave him this LOOK, when he acted
like
He ain't heard...Dat particular look, we black mens have
Learned to master WITHOUT usin words....

But he ain't even impressed. & he AIN'T backin down
What was he, stoopid? Then he put his patent-leather foot
Down, "LOOK, I TOLD YOU! I DON'T WANT ANY SHIT!
THIS IS YOUR LAST WARNING.   (Silence) OKAY, THAT'S
IT!"

But I play to win.   Be a homeboy in full!   Did he know who
He wuz fuckin wit? Enuf of dis bullshit!
Homey had all he could take...& would take no mo!

"LOOK MAN, I DUN TOLD YOU ONCE...
I PAID MY WAY ABOARD
DIS HELLHOLE A LONG TIME AGO!
NOW GIT THE HELL OUT OF MY FACE!

Now he snarls dat way they do. Like you are the filthiest,
Lowest, stank, rancid, piece of shit pollutin the planet...
& he really HATES you...really don't even wanna talk to you
But it was part of the gig, so what else could he do?

"NO, YOU HAVEN'T PAID, DAMMIT! YOU PAY ME RIGHT

NOW...OR YOU CAN PAY THE METRO POLICE!"
"YO! READ MY NEGROID LIPS! I PAID!
CALL THE MAN! SHIT!
CALL YO MAMA,
YOU UPPITY SHANK-BREATH-RACIST-MUTHAFUCKA!"

& all the blue eyes sucked their teeth at me, silently, but
I can hear it. Hell, I can smell the foul winds from it!

The train HALTS! It's Fordham Station. This is not, repeat
NOT my destination! But the man is waitin to take me away,
Again. The man with the executioner eyes and hangman's smile
(Y'all know the one) The man stands, nightstick in hand
All fired-up & ready to kick my nappy ass all over the South
Bronx, & send me home, mo "nigguh," than I was yesterday...

But not 1/2 the bug-eyed-whipped-&-circumsized maimed-crippled
History-wild dog chow-fire-hosed-bullet-ridden-afro-explodin-
"nigguh"...I'll be tomorrow, if somebody DARES to tell ME...
I ain't Paid...MY FARE?!

SHHHHHIIIIIIT!▲

Marlon D. Satchell Energetic best describes Marlon Satchell. The talented student at the Baldwin School for girls makes time for reading, writing, swimming, rowing, drawing, ballet and eating. Marlon enthusiastically aspires to pursue a career in science. She was born in Lower Merion, PA on February 13, 1977. Currently Marlon lives in Philadelphia, PA with her family including their family pet Poo Tzu.

"It's time we stop listening to our pockets and start listening to our hearts." ▲

➤ *Velvet Blanket* ➤

A haunting velvet blanket
smothers the moon in her darkness.
And for a single moment
there is only the smooth, satiating darkness,
and the eerie sigh of the breeze.
No motion, no light, no moon.
But only for a second.
then her blanket of velvet disappears.▲

➤ *Grandfather Grandfather*➤

I remember...
Sitting on his lap
Leaning against his big round tummy
His big smiling face
He was so much fun...
But he died when we were both so young. ▲

Sharan Strange, 32, was born in Heidelberg, Germany and grew up in Orangeburg, SC. She was educated at Harvard University where she currently works in studio arts administration. She is co-founder of the Dark Room Writers Collective and is co-editor of *Muleteeth*. Her work has appeared in several journals and she is at work on a volume of poetry. ▲

➤ *Transits* ➤

I.
Once Father raised
a broom to me—before
possibility moved in me
like blood, wouldn't flow, just
backed up
on itself, a sluggish creek—
& raised a purple welt
across my cheek.

2.
It didn't happen
on my 14th birthday
like Mama thought,
but a month before
during Sunday service, I stumbled
down, down
to the tiny basement toilet, as
a red-orange map defined itself
on my underwear. Is that how God
claimed Mary? Did she first bleed
in His house?

3.
At this age,
or before,
I am henceforth liable
for my sins.
His left hand
covering my heart,
my minister slapped
his right palm hard
against my forehead,
set off flares & blood
erupting. Through vertigo,
talk of cleansing.

4.
My husband gone
a year—child too—this
scar reminds me.
Each month I still bleed.
I also refuse
my Father's house.
I intend to keep
on doing so.▲

➤ *Streetcorner Church* ➤

Is grace delivered
on twilight wings of air?
Don't ask this congregation.
They'd shout *"Yes!"*
then breathe mightily
to draw you in.

A speaker strapped
to a car roof floats
gospel—a curbside choir-in-the-box.
Graffiti-scored stone for pews.
The ceiling dispatches
prayer straight upstairs.
Dubious oasis; Jesus might've shed
bitter tears here.

Three would-be saints
in red-soaked garb stroll by,
mockingly sound the refrain:
"Sinner, won't you come?"
The sun seeps burgundy,
gone-to-glory behind the altar.
The humming air of deliverance
lingers like a whore's perfume.▲

➤Acts of Power➤

At 8,
the magnets of my fickle thoughts
were three; school, boys & play.
They gave me furlough from home's cell.
At school, I pleased benevolent wardens
with mathematical & verbal skill.

                                    Boys
were mine to climb trees with, hunt
blackberries & plums, plot strategy
in simulated war. One boy, my brother,
tirelessly taunted me in games of tag.
He'd let me come *this close* before
springing out of reach...

                                    Play
went on mostly inside my head. I
devised a life that appeased some inner
god, that plucked a wire in me to sound
I AM & released me from the stasis
of numb things. It spun me out like a top,
dancing to the world's bright limits; then,
responding to a rhythm arbitrary & true,
arced me back to the axis, communal core.

                                    I sat
in a field among tall green reeds whose
cayenne-colored tips waved like anemone.
We'd suck the salty juices from the stalks—
taste of our thirsting bodies, taste of
the source of life, the sea.

                                    Drunk
on their tears, I ran toward home
and in the road between collided
with the sudden car. Rebellious brakes
halted it—no, I! It sent me hurtling,
a sprung torpedo singing home. The machine
acceded to a force more delicate
& braver than its own. ▲

➤ *Barbershop Ritual* ➤

Baby brother can't wait.
For him, the rite of passage
begins early—before obligatory heists
of candy & comic books from neighborhood
stores, before street battles to claim
turf, before he might gain
the title "Man of the House"
before his time.

Each week, he steps up to the chair,
the closest semblance of a throne
he'll ever know, and lays in
for the cut, the counseling of
older dudes, cappin' players, men-of-words,
Greek chorus to the comic-tragic fanfare
of approaching manhood.

Baby brother's named for two fathers,
and each Saturday he seeks them
in this neutral zone of brotherhood,
where manhood sprouts like new growth
week by week and dark hands
deftly shape identity.

Head-bowed, church-solemn,
he sheds hair like motherlove & virginity,
weightier than Air Jordans & designer
sweats—euphemistic battle gear.
He receives the tribal standard:
a nappy helmet sporting arrows, lightening
bolts, rows of lines cut in—New World
scarification—or carved logos (Adidas,
Public Enemy) and tags, like hieroglyphic
distress signs to the ancestors:
Remember us, remember our names!▲

➤ *The Crazy Girl* ➤

She was given to fits,
so was her brother.
There was a category
for him. *Retarded,* they said.
Something nearer to sin named her.

Oh, the family claimed
its share of deviance—inbreeding,
generation after generation
of drunks, rootworkers, thieves,
feuds carried on with
the extravagant viciousness of kin.

But hers was an unpredictable
violence—more disturbing because
she wasn't a man, besides
being a child. So they settled
on puberty—the mysterious workings
of female hormones—until she
outgrew it and the moniker stuck.

It accounted for the rage
worn on her face, tight as
a fist, fear and restlessness in eyes
like July 4th's slaughtered pig.
Rebellious, wooly hair only
partly tamed by braids, she often
inflicted pain during play.
Boys her favorite victims,
she tore clothes, skin,
marked virgin expanses of face, neck, arms
with scratches like filigreed monograms.

Her notoriety was assured when,
at 16, she disappeared, leaving
rumor to satisfy the family's need
to understand, giving context to

her uncle's slow slide into madness,
her sullen body bruised by constant
scratching, as if she could
somehow remove his touch.▲

Patrick Sylvain, born in Port-au-Prince, Haiti on June 12, 1966. Migrated to Boston, MA in December 1981. Education: B.A. in political science and social psychology from the University of Massachusetts at Boston. Currently working on M.A. and M.Ed.; Occupation: Bilingual teacher at the Robert F. Kennedy School in Cambridge. Hobbies: photography and videography. Member of the Dark Room Writers Collective, extremely active in Haitian and Third World politics. Basically, I live for and learn from the people, and love poetry.

Patrick is published in the following: *American Poetry Anthology, Howth Castle, Haiti Progress, Haiti en Marche, Mass Media, Moody Street Review, Muleteeth, New Strategy* and *Prisma.*

"None but ourselves can free our mind/have no fear for atomic energy 'cause none of them can stop the time/how long shall they kill our prophets/while we stand aside and look.... (Redemption Song)."–Bob Marley▲

➤ *Collective Search* ➤

I am a word hunter,
hunted by words.
I seek words to demystify cosmetic atrocities.
Sometimes I wish words could gush
out of my tongue like water
freed from congested pipes.

My friend with his "uncombed universe"
is an Inkslinger—
his pen is loaded Go-Go word gun.

Humpty Dumpty is bounty
dancing marionettes on her ears,
words seep through a tiny gap
between her teeth landing on white pages
appearing in front of a thousand eyes.

"Groovy Dreads" is a Be-Bop swinger
a lyrical poet
rhythm and words groove at the tip of her pen
like Monk's fingers on blue notes
her words entice movements
groove
come on groove.

The lady with "kissed knees"
writes words inside washer machines
and observes images bubbled
into speculative stories.

Keene the evergreen
commands an army of words
into satirical characters.

Our eyes are on every shelf
dusting off blacks' names
for the Dark Room

where hundreds of eyes and ears
gather to cultivate worlds.

From Jazz to Blues
Go-Go to Funk
Reggae to African Rumba
sculptures to pictures;
culture is our pulse.

We are hunted by words,
we hunt words to explore our inner worlds.

Our eyes have seen a world of art
hundreds of faces craving for culture makers
ears attending to words
like Christians waiting for benedictions.

Books laid siege
upon the walls and the floor.
Our eyes are constant decoders;
we collect what word makers produce.
We are word hunters
and we are hunted by words,
our culture, ourselves. ▲

➤ *Constant Memories* ➤

I read in unforgettable books
the ceaseless action of water
which brought to shore
hunters of eternity and
lovers of death ecstasy.

How can you ask me to be
silent in this twilight
when terror of the past
dances in my mind?

All that hunting
and the terror
staring straight from Indians' eyes
like the sun shimmering on water.

Columbus' virtues were vices in disguise.
His name knocks on us like bells,
his discovery our burial ground.
What is there for me to celebrate?

The sea brings bad memories
and Christopher Columbus is a constant hawk
lurking in the back of conscious minds.
His memory is the stench of hell.

1492 was an eternal death festivity
with blood dripping in mining fields,
in hawks' beaks
and in between lovers thighs.
How can I be silent in this twilight of terror? ▲

➤ *Panama* ➤

When death crawls by night

on a spider's back

and lives inside a brother's

shirt pocket

like a handkerchief,

life,

through the eyes of

the Eagle, is seen as

the Lamb ready to be clawed.▲

Andrea M. Wren, 23, is a native of East St. Louis, IL, a graduate of Spelman College and the 1990 recipient of the Zora Neale Hurston-Langston Hughes Award made possible by Alice Walker. Her work has appeared in *Catalyst, Drumvoices Revue, The Original Chicago Blues Annual* and *Word Up: Black Poetry of the 80's from the Deep South.*▲

➤*Harmony*➤

i would like for ebony and ivory
to live together
in harmony.
but i'm tired of white girls
harmonizing
with black men—
playing the "sax"
and singing the blues
in non-
musical ways.▲

➤A Day At School➤

Go t' School
Come Late
Smoke Pot
Drink Booze
Get High
Fight Teach
Bell Rings
Open Door
Gun Shot
Brother's Dead
School's Out▲

➤ Surrogate Mothers ➤

the night sighs
as it finally embraces its last child.
the children all safe at home
settle down for their nightly meal
suckling at the breast of their mother
secure in the knowledge that the milk
is pure.

one child nestles in the arms of love
and goes to sleep
as the shadows of darkness dance
and the child cooscontent
as another track is added to her arm.

as the child lies in the bosom of serenity
with her head lying on dirty syringes,
the night sobs
as another one of her children is embraced
and loved
by a surrogate mother. ▲

FICTION

Confounding the author who is trying to lay his cards on the
table is the dogging knowledge that his imagination is a kind
of community medium of exchange....Yet the author is eager to
explain.

—Richard Wright

SUGAR THANG

by JABARI ASIM

jabari asim his photo and bio appear in the poetry section.▲

Schoolboy glanced at his Piaget watch. "Damn," he said. "It's only three o'clock. You mean to tell me you won't have another flight until tomorrow morning? I got an appointment tomorrow morning."

The blonde ticket agent was polite but efficient. "Sorry, Sir, but Paducah isn't exactly a bustling metropolis. It would not be very cost-efficient to schedule more than one flight per day."

Schoolboy let his cigarette dangle from his lips. "No offense, but St. Louie ain't exactly a bustling metropolis either, and there are flights comin' in and out of here all goddamn day!"

He removed his Vuarnet shades and wiped them clean with the tip of his Geoffrey Beene pocket square. Just great, Schoolboy thought. I have to stay all night in this backward burg. If I had known this was going to happen I would have spent another night in Chi-town.

Let's see. I'll come back tomorrow, fly to Paducah, finalize the deal, then drive to Cairo. I'll have plenty of time to prepare for my date with Rhonda. Ah, yes, Rhonda. A former Miss Black Illinois. If all goes right she'll be screaming my name 'til sunrise. Meanwhile, I'd better make the most of my current situation. Rent a room and a car and hit the streets.

Schoolboy leaned forward and flicked a piece of paper from his Florsheims before stepping into his rented Trans Am. While styling down highway 70, he thought of what he'd heard about St. Louis. His college classmates from there had referred to it as a "country city." To hear them tell it, the Gateway City had never grown up. Folks still walked around barefoot, talked backward, and grew collard greens in their backyards. Well, Schoolboy mused, you can take niggers out of the country . . . .

He turned off at an exit leading to the black side of town, hoping to find a restaurant. He had a McDonald's in mind, but the name of a greasy spoon caught his eye: Stockbroker's Barbershop and Grill.

That's strange, he thought. Maybe they mean *bar* and grill. And where'd they get a name like Stockbroker's? Only one way to find out.

Schoolboy backed the Trans Am into a nearby space.

He walked to the shop's entrance and stepped in. The room consisted of two huge, throne-like barber chairs, a wash basin behind each of them, and a long wall mirror. The floor was decorated with a checkerboard pattern of faded red and white tiles.

There were three men inside. The first man, apparently the barber, sat on one of the thrones reading a newspaper. The second man sat in a folding chair, engaged in a solitary checker game. The third man sat at a shoe-shine stand in the corner, humming softly.

"Afternoon," Schoolboy said. "Is the grill open?"

"In about ten minutes," the barber said. He nodded toward an ancient refrigerator at the back of the room. "Grab a cool drink and have a sit-down."

"Don't mind if I do."

Schoolboy took a bottle of Orange Whistle from the refrigerator, opened it, and took a swallow. He sat down next to the man playing checkers. From there he could see the doorway leading to the grill. He could hear the clatter of dishes and splashing water.

Each of the men had ceased his respective activity. All were looking expectantly. He shifted in his seat. "Name's Schoolboy," he said. "I'm a salesman from Chicago. Just here for the night."

"Salesman, huh? That's good, Ah guess . . . Ahm Stockbroker. Ah own this place." Stockbroker was a tall, thin, white-haired man with a long face that was both sad and aristocratic. He looked like a judge who sentenced all his defendants to death, yet pitied them at the same time.

The man beside Schoolboy spoke next. He wore a plaid shirt with pinstriped suspenders. "Ahm called Misery," he said. He pulled a harmonica from his pocket and waved it about with a flourish. "And Ahm a musician."

Y-You-You, a-ain't no, musician," the third man said. "Y-You j-just think y-you one." The stutterer was a rail-thin man with a concave chest. His few remaining teeth were brown and rotten. He wore an old baseball cap and a pair of extremely thick eyeglasses.

"Shut up, Sweet Pea!" Misery thundered. "What d' *you* know? Sheeit, when Ah was a boy Ah taught Freddie Green how t' play guitar."

"Right," Stockbroker said with a dry grin that was close to a grimace. "And Ah played ball with Cool Papa Bell."

"Uh-huh, that's right. Mess with me if you want," Misery said. He turned to Schoolboy. "Do you listen t' the blues, Salesman?"

"Uh, yeah, I like blues. And that's Schoolboy. The name's Schoolboy."

"Whatever," Misery said. "Name a musician you like."

"I like Bob James, David Sanborn."

"Figgers. And you don't even know John Lee Hooker, do ya?"

"Sure I do. He's a shortstop. Now if you'll excuse me, I—"

Suddenly a voice cried out, "Grill's open."

Schoolboy heard the voice and laughed inside himself. It was a voice like a cool drink on a hot summer day. That, he thought, is the voice of a beautiful woman, which explains why I came in here in the first place. Good ol' intuition. You haven't let me down yet.

"Like I was saying, I believe dinner is being served." Schoolboy rose, grabbed his soda, stole a glance at himself in the mirror and entered the diner.

Schoolboy was right. The voice he'd heard belonged to a woman who was absolutely stunning. A thin film of sweat adorned her sculptured cheekbones. Her long, wooly hair was pulled back in a single, fat braid. She wore a sleeveless blouse that was tied at the waist and cut-off shorts that looked molded to her fabulous black body. Every swell and curve was beautifully obvious: the perfect ripeness of her breasts, the gentle slope of her belly, the exquisite roundness of her buttocks.

When Schoolboy sat down at the counter he couldn't help but notice the laughter in her eyes, the promise in her lips.

Jesus God almighty damn, he thought. Schoolboy felt strangely out of breath. Accustomed to pretentious, heavily-painted women, he was bowled over by her natural, timeless beauty. He figured she would look just as good, just as natural, beside the banks of the Kamby Bolongo, or in a Mississippi cotton field.

"Hello," he said.

"Hi," she replied.

"My name's Schoolboy."

"Mine's Goodie. How'd you get a name like Schoolboy?"

"It's a nickname. Because I'm smart. How about you?"

Goodie giggled. "Mine's a nickname too. Only Ah ain't smart. Ahm good. What'll ya have?"

"I'll have a burger. Naw, wait. Can you handle chicken-fried steak?"

"Best in the state."

"Well, I'll have that, and fries. Whatcha got for dessert?"

Goodie leaned closer. "How 'bout somethin' black and sweet and juicy?"

"Are we talking about what I think we're talking about?"

"Yeah, if you think we talkin' 'bout blackberry pie."

Goodie went to work. She got out flour, pepper, onion powder, salt and an egg. She whipped the egg, then she got out a steak, pounded it, and dipped it into the egg, then the flour mixture.

"So Schoolboy" she said. "You a propah talkin' man. Where you from?"

"Chicago. And you?"

"Ahm from Mobile."

"I guess they're still crying in Mobile."

"Whatcha mean?"

"I mean if I lived in Mobile, and you left, I'd probably never get over it."

"Aw, you sweet. But Ah don't think they miss me too much."

Goodie emptied the bowl that she'd beaten the egg in and plunged it into an enormous tub of dishwater. Most of the suds were already dead; a thin skin of gray scum covered the water's surface. Goodie took her time, as if she knew Schoolboy was watching her ass. At last she returned to the counter.

She leaned forward, allowing Schoolboy to fasten his gaze on her breasts. Um, he thought. Bet those nipples swell up to silver dollar size.

I'm going to pop them into my mouth like plums.

He looked up and found her eyes. Schoolboy felt that she was testing him, daring him, saying, "Come and get it. If you're bad enough."

Goodie licked her lips, then turned away.

"Where are you going?" Schoolboy asked.

"Where it look like Ahm going"? T' start up yo' fries."

"As long as you don't go too far. My heart couldn't take it. Give me another soda, will you?"

Schoolboy finished his first soda and put the second bottle to his lips. When he put it down he found Goodie staring at him thoughtfully, her moist lips slightly curved.

"What's on your mind?" he asked.

"Aw, just thinkin'."

"About?"

Goodie's smile grew wider. "Well, Ah was just thinkin' that Ah know what a man look like when he like what he lookin' at."

"And?"

"You got that look."

"You're very perceptive."

"Ah been called a lotta things, but Ah don't think Ah evah been called that. What it mean?"

Good Lord, Schoolboy mused. A child's mind trapped in the body of a goddess. This is going to be easier than taking land from a nigger.

"It means, dear lady, that you know what you're seeing when you're looking at something. Or someone."

"Know somethin', Schoolboy?"

"What?"

"You sho' talk funny."

"So you think I'm funny, eh?" Schoolboy reached out and stroked Goodie's hand. "What else do you think about me?"

Goodie studied him for a moment, then giggled and pulled away. "Ah betta check on yo' steak."

Women are the same wherever you go, Schoolboy thought as he watched Goodie move. Even the stupid ones like to play games.

Goodie pulled a small salad from the refrigerator and placed it on the counter. Schoolboy took careful notice of the graceful, taunt muscles working smoothly beneath her sleek, dark skin.

"So," he said. "What's the story about this place?"

Goodie removed the steak from the skillet and flipped it onto a plate. She put two slices of buttered bread next to the steak and put the dish on the counter. "What do you mean?" she asked.

"I mean, what about those old characters in the other room? And what made Stockbroker combine a barbershop and diner?"

"They used to be two different places. This was Wynonie's Good Time Grill. 'Nonie won the lottery and moved to New Orleans, so Stock knocked a hole in the wall and took it over."

"What about Misery and Sweet Pea?"

"Misery just hangs around. He don't mean no harm. When his mama was pregnant with him, his daddy ran away and left her in misery. That's how he got his name. Sweet Pea was in the war. Whatcha call it when you in the army and you run away."

"You go AWOL. You're a deserter."

"Yeah, right. Sweet Pea did it and they caught 'im and did 'speriments on 'im. He been touched evah since."

"Damn! No shit?"

"The NAACP took it t' court, but the judge threw it out. His brother take care of 'im, an' he shine shoes for Stockbroker."

"Some story. I'm sorry I asked . . . Do you get much business?"

"Most times it slow. Hardly nobody come in. Then, sometimes it look like we just *pull* people in. How's that steak?"

"Juicy. Like I like it, know what I mean?"

Goodie just smiled. "Don't eat too fast," she cautioned. "You might git a upset stomach."

"Don't worry, baby," Schoolboy replied. "I don't do anything fast. I do everything real slow."

"Ooh, you so bad."

"And, you're so good. So what are we going to do?"

Just then Stockbroker, Misery and Sweet Pea entered the diner. They sat down next to Schoolboy.

"Do you fellows mind?" Schoolboy hinted. "The lady and I are having a private conversation."

"What y'all want?" Goodie added. "Ain'tcha got no heads t' cut? No shoes t' shine?"

"Nope," Stockbroker answered, never taking his eyes off Schoolboy. "Business is slow. 'Sides, you got company, Goodie."

Schoolboy turned and nearly choked on his steak when he saw the giant stride in.

"S-St-Stiff!" Sweet Pea exclaimed.

"Sweet Pea!" the giant responded. "What's the word, everybody?"

"Hey, Stiff, how you feel?" Misery asked.

"Afternoon, Stiff," Stockbroker added with a solemn nod.

Stiff was about 6'4", Schoolboy figured. His hair was cut close to his head, which rested on a neck of Herculean proportions. He wore a tee-shirt and khaki work pants, neither of which seemed able to contain his abundant muscles. Stiff had large, clear eyes and a ready smile. He resembled a large stone sculpture come to life.

Stiff grinned at Goodie. "How's my sugar thang today?"

Goodie smiled bashfully. "Fine," she answered.

"Don't know if she's still yo' sugar thang, Stiff," Misery said. He pointed at Schoolboy. "Ah'd say you got some competition."

Stiff noticed Schoolboy for the first time. "Hello," he said. "Name's Stiff."

"Nice to meet you, Stiff," Schoolboy said while extending his hand. "I'm Schoolboy."

"Schoolboy's a salesman," Goodie said. "He just passin' through."

Stiff gripped Schoolboy's hand and eyed him warily. "Salesman, huh?"

"Yeah," Schoolboy answered, sensing that Stiff had already sized him up and dismissed him. He tried to sound friendly and unconcerned. "What do *you* do?"

"I chop down trees for the city." Stiff flexed his mountainous bicep. "Sometimes I use an ax."

What a joke, Schoolboy thought. You muscle-headed idiot. Don't you know you're playing with fire? I was always king of the dozens, even as a boy. I'll cut you down as easily as you chop down trees.

"Very impressive," Schoolboy said. "But you should use an ax more often. It'll save your head lots of wear and tear."

The others laughed, except Misery. He pointed a stubby finger at Schoolboy. "Ah'd shut m' gums if Ah was you. You gittin' in ovah yo' head."

"Mind yo' own business, Misery!" Stiff barked. "This is between me and him." Stiff regained control of himself. Once again he became the smiling giant. "Look," he said in almost gentle tones, "Goodie says you're just passin' through. Why don't you just go on and do that. I don't like my lady bein' bothered by strangers."

"She never said she was your lady."

"You callin' me a liar?"

"I'm just telling you that she never said that." Schoolboy looked at the old men. Something in their faces reminded him of Romans and gladiator matches.

"The way I see it," Stiff began, "you're callin' me a liar. I don't like that. You been botherin' my sugar thang, and I don't like that either. You want somethin' that belongs t' me and I ain't about t' give it t' you. Only way you gon' git it is t' take it. It's on you, Salesman. I'm callin' you out."

Schoolboy looked at Stiff and considered the challenge. Shit, he thought, his arm is bigger than my whole body. Schoolboy turned and looked at Goodie, who was suddenly busy cleaning the grill. Yeah, she's fine, he conceded, but there are plenty of fine bitches in the world, none of whom I am willing to get my ass kicked for. If she wants to spend her time with Mandingo, that's cool. I'll just slide while the night is still young.

"Relax, man. I don't want your woman."

Stiff looked disappointed. "Then, you don't want t' fight?"

"Naw. Just forget it."

"Well, let me ask you somethin'. Your mouth taste funny?"

"No. Why?"

Stiff scratched his jaw thoughtfully. "I just figured your mouth might taste funny, seein' how you just kissed my ass and all."

Before Schoolboy could respond, Stiff casually extended his foot and nudged his rival from his seat and onto the floor. "Make a move, Salesman," Stiff commanded.

Schoolboy could no longer see the twisted faces of the old men, or Goodie's sensual curves. He only saw a grinning giant taking up all the space in the world. I *knew* I should've gone to McDonald's, he thought. Okay. Time to put all that Nautilus training to work. I'm going to get up, fake left, cut right and fly out the door. Then I'll get into my ride and drive the hell away. If I ever get stranded in St. Louis again, I'm going straight back to Chi-town, even if I have to *crawl.*

Schoolboy rose quickly, but Stiff was quicker. He shoved Schoolboy against the counter. Schoolboy grabbed his soda bottle and smashed it on the counter's edge. Not bad so far, he thought.

He waved his jagged weapon at Stiff. "Don't make me slice you," he hissed. Stiff laughed and swatted the bottle from Schoolboy's hand. He grabbed Schoolboy by the throat and sent him hurtling over the counter. Schoolboy slammed against the refrigerator before sliding to the floor.

The force of the impact manifested itself in frightening bursts of pain the length of Schoolboy's spine. He felt as if someone had shattered a cattleprod and buried the buzzing segments in his skull. Schoolboy regained his focus just in time to see Stiff hurdling the counter. "Look, man," he said, but Stiff only chuckled. He lifted Schoolboy and shoved him head-first into the dishpan.

"Chrissakes," Misery said. "Look like you killin' that boy."

"Serve him right," Stockbroker said. "Man like that deserve t' die, tryin' t' talk t' anotha man's gal."

Stiff pulled Schoolboy's head from the dishpan and held him by the scruff of his neck. "You ain't never lied, Stock," he said. "You ain't never lied."

Coughing, spitting and choking, Schoolboy felt as if his head was being pulled inside out. His ears, eyes and nose were full of water.

"That ain't all he done," Goodie said.

Stiff looked up. "Whatcha talkin' bout?"

"Uh, he tried t' feel on me, that's what he done."

"I'll be damned," Stiff exclaimed. He shoved Schoolboy back into the suds with a swift movement of his mighty hand. Then gripped Schoolboy's

his feet and swayed uncertainly. Sweet Pea rushed to him.

"H-Hey, Salesman, you . . . alright?"

Schoolboy angrily shook Sweet Pea off, limped painfully to a washbasin and gripped it with both hands.

"A-Ah was j-just tryin' t' h-help," Sweet Pea muttered.

"Leave 'im 'lone, Pea!" Stockbroker hollered. "He got hisself inta trouble, he can git hisself out."

Schoolboy did not recognize himself in the mirror. His once handsome features had ballooned into a grotesque parody of a face. His eyes were mere puffy slits; his split, bloated lips were caked with dried blood. All for a piece of ass, Schoolboy thought. He sneaked a look at the grill's entrance. The door was shut. He turned and slowly scanned the interior of the barbershop. Only the three old men were present.

"Lookin' for Stiff?" Misery asked. "Ah wouldn't worry 'bout him none. He busy gittin hisself somethin' good. Somethin' you wish you nevah laid eyes on."

"Looked good enough t' eat, didn't she boy?" Stockbroker asked. "Only this time you bit off more 'n you could chew."

The three men began to laugh, which only increased Schoolboy's humiliation and pain. I *must* get the hell out of here, he thought. He staggered to the door and twisted the knob with both hands, working his fingertips in a frenzied, desparate motion, as if he were trying to unscrew a hot light bulb.

He staggered outside and stepped gingerly to his car. After painfully retrieving his keys from his pocket, he opened the door and fell in. Sweat rolled into his eyes and burned with a stubborn insistence as he started the engine. He felt his consciousness fading, his mind dissolving into distorted dreams of promising lips and black, glistening thighs. A hospital, Schoolboy thought . . . . Uh, to get some help . . . Help . . . He steered his car on to the avenue.

There was a knock at the door. "Don't tell me that fool salesman came back," Misery said. "Everybody else know you closed."

"T-Think it's m' brotha," Sweet Pea said. "He comin' t' git me."

Stockbroker rose from his throne and peeped through the glass. "Yep. It's Frank."

Stockbroker opened the door. "Hey, Frank, come on in. Leave the do' open. Hot in here anyway."

"How's everybody?" Frank asked. He was a tall, straight-backed, good-natured fellow. He turned to his brother.

"All set, Sweet Pea?"

"Y-Yeah, F-Frank. Ah'm . . . ready."

"Alright, then. Let's hit the road, Jack . . . . Y'all hear 'bout the accident under the overpass?"

hair and pulled him out of the water.

Stiff slowly shook his head. "I was gonna let him off easy, but I cain't let people think they can go around feelin' on my woman."

"Right, Stiff," Misery agreed. "A man does somethin' like that is only gittin' what he deserve."

Stiff cradled Schoolboy's head in his palm. He made a fist with his free hand and began hammering Schoolboy's face with short, staccato punches. He pummelled Schoolboy beyond unconsciousness, until a thin sheen of sweat formed on his muscular brow.

"That's enough, Stiff," Goodie suggested. Stiff stopped and looked at her. The room was silent except for the labored, eager gasps of the old men. Goodie smiled. "Come on, sweetie. Ah think he learned his lesson."

"But, baby," Stiff objected, "you said he tried t' feel on you. I was just gittin' started."

Goodie laughed. "But watchin' those muscles of yours done got *me* started. Ah was hopin' *you'd* come feel on me. But Ah guess you busy."

"Hell naw!" Stiff shouted. "Some things a man ain't never too busy for." He dropped Schoolboy and reached Goodie in a single bound.

He laughed and pulled her to him. Goodie moaned as Stiff kissed her. She ground her hips against him until he began to squeeze and rub her buttocks. Stiff stopped suddenly.

"Who the hell do y'all think y'all are?" he bellowed. "Give us some privacy, goddammit. Take that salesman with ya."

Misery and Stockbroker dragged Schoolboy into the barbershop. Sweet Pea lingered and looked hopefully at Stiff. Stiff sighed and waved him away. "You, too, Pea. Go on and scram. That's it, go 'head."

Sweet Pea shuffled reluctantly to the door, then turned and looked at Stiff, his cloudy eyes brimming with tears. Stiff's voice grew soft. "Not t'night, Pea. Maybe some other time, okay?"

"O-Okay," Sweet Pea sobbed. Misery returned and pulled him roughly through the door. "Stop blubberin', ya old fool?" he shouted. "Ya cain't expect 'im t' let us watch *all* the time, can ya? Keep that up 'n' he ain't nevah gon' let us watch no mo'. Then watcha' gon' do, huh?"

Schoolboy woke suddenly. He tried to jerk himself up but found that quickness was an impossibility. As simple a movement as a blink of his eyes caused electric fingers of pain to grip his entire body. When the room stopped spinning he saw Sweet Pea standing over him with an empty bucket in his hands.

"Give 'im anotha shot, Pea," Misery instructed.

"N-Naw," Sweet Pea replied. "Ah . . . Ah think he's c-comin' out of it."

Schoolboy discovered that he could hardly move anything, including his tongue, which was immersed in blood. He was certain that several teeth were loose and reasonably sure that his jaw was broken. He rose slowly to

"We heard the sireens and all," Misery answered. "Figgered it was a smash-up. Was it one of those young fools on dope?"

"Nope," Frank said. He pulled a stick of Doublemint out of his pocket, carefully unwrapped it, put it in his mouth and chewed it thoughtfully. "Some fella lost control of his car and crossed the middle line. Hit a station wagon and ended up wrapped around a concrete pillar. Everybody dead as doornails. Ya know, maybe the fella was drunk."

"Was he black or white?" Stockbroker asked.

"Aw, he was black alright. My nephew saw it all. Said when they pulled him out, he looked like he been fifteen rounds with Mike Tyson. The police said the fella was some kinda salesman."

"D-Dirty shame," Sweet Pea added. He turned to Misery. "Y-You think—-?"

"Yeah," Misery quickly replied, "Ah think ya right. It sho' is a dirty shame. Shame, Ah guess, any time somebody die."

"That's what peoples is born fo'," Stockbroker mused as he lit a cigar and began to puff lazy, billowing circles into the air.

"What's that you say?" Frank asked.

"Ah said, that's what peoples is born fo'. T' die."

"Gospel truth ya speakin'," Misery added. "Sho' 'nuff righteous gospel truth." Then he fished his harmonica from his pocket and blew a long, mournful note. It twisted slowly out of the barbershop door and climbed into the deep, black sky.▲

Valerie Boyd Born December 11, 1963, Valerie Boyd is the founder, editor and publisher of *EightRock*, an Atlanta-based but world-centered magazine of African-American arts and culture. She is also the assistant editor of *Catalyst*, an Atlanta-based literary magazine. To support her love for creative journalism, truth-telling fiction, innovative arts and drylongso black culture, she also works as an editor at *The Atlanta Journal-Constitution*. For more information on *EightRock* (subscriptions are $10 for four issues), write to P.O. Box 144, Atlanta, GA 30301.▲

THREE

by VALERIE BOYD

Adele's hands were folded awkwardly across the pages of the large, open textbook. She sat in the dark with only an architect's lamp lighting the pages and her hands. The moonlight, streaming in through the open window, cast a blue glow on her face. She felt stifled, claustrophobic, languid. Perhaps it's the heat, she thought, staring into nowhere. A warm breeze stirred the thin blue curtains, but the hot breath of the Chicago summer did not move Adele's troubled face and unfocused eyes. "Perhaps it's the heat," she whispered to herself.

She listened to the mechanical sounds of the stereo as the record player dropped another disc onto the turntable. She called it a stereo, but it was a phonograph, the old-fashioned 1970s kind that allowed you to stack the records and wait for them to drop. Hours of continuous music, thanks to the foresight, pack-ratness and thoughtfulness of her Aunt Joan, who had given her the phonograph when she had first gone off to college. She could remember the day when Joan presented it to her. That—along with the overnight bag that Ms. Smith, her favorite high school teacher, had given her—was her favorite, most sensible graduation gift. It seemed like such a long time ago, but it had only been a couple of years. But so much had happened since then.

"A velvet shade of blue
I search for you.
But all I visualize is time on my hands."

The lonely contralto, at first just a rustle, sang from Adele's miniature stereo speakers. Then the supple voice, sweeter than honey, filled the room, and the song rushed to Adele's head, a bittersweet assault.

"The bedroom dark,
The kitchen cold
The clock reminds me I got time on my hands."

As if awaking from a trance, Adele clicked off the light in a sudden, spastic movement. Then, wearily, she laid her head down on her hands. Only the blue-tinted light from the open window caressed her face.

****

As Beverly and Omari entered the Black Student Union building, it occurred to Beverly that she was tired, even though they hadn't even begun to study. She was tired from hours, days and weeks of trying to squeeze conversation out of Omari. But it was easier than the alternative.

Beverly continued to try to be talkative and lovey-dovey but Omari was aloof, preoccupied with other thoughts. Occasionally, he attempted to be kind and show some interest in whatever Beverly was saying, for he was not without love for her.

****

The couple sat in a large room inside the converted house, Beverly was draped casually across a chair a short distance from Omari, who was lying on the couch. They shared a comfortable and knowing silence, punctuated occasionally by the recitation of an irresistible passage from the separate books they were consuming. The solitude allowed Beverly to hear a rustling footsteps in the distance.

Adele mounted the steps of the old house slowly, tentatively, her mouth moving as though she was singing to herself. Her eyes were distant.

Beverly's breath quickened as she heard the door of the building open. She swallowed hard.

Adele stepped into the open doorway of the room, waved and mumbled "hi." Beverly and Omari looked up briefly, returned Adele's greeting and went back to their silent reading. Adele sat at a table between Beverly and Omari. Her back against the wall, she faced the couple, opened a large textbook and joined them in silent reading.

Soon, Beverly got up, walked to the patio door and looked out into the darkness. Restless, she stepped out onto the porch, struggling to keep her head still, looking straight ahead. She felt the impulse to turn her head and look over her shoulder, back into the room where Adele and Omari were in the beginnings of a pleasant conversation that animated Adele like Beverly had rarely seen her. Beverly clenched her teeth and tensed her neck to stop her head from turning around to bear witness.

Agitated, she walked further onto the porch and paced around uncomfortably in the night air. I wish I had a cigarette, she thought. Beverly didn't even smoke. But, If I'm going to be pacing around on this porch, I'd look a lot cooler if I had a cigarette, she thought. She laughed at the thought, a bitter taste in her mouth.

She walked listlessly to the porch's ledge and sat down, folding her arms across her chest, resting her back on a column of the porch. The wood felt cool against her back, offering refuge from the oppressive heat inside the room—the heat of the boring June night; the heat of Adele's presence, her intrusion into the room. Although Adele and Beverly had forged an uneasy peace, Beverly still felt banished from the room by her presence.

Beverly hugged herself and sighed heavily. The sound of the chirping crickets and a lone passing car comforted her. But, like the blues, the soft laughter from inside the room was music to her ears. Peering through the clouds in her eyes, she gazed up at the stars.

Beverly was lost in her thoughts. How could she return to the room with the two of them sitting there? Adele simply replacing Beverly, taking Beverly's place in the room, so quickly and unapologetically, just as she had done briefly in Omari's life. How could Beverly return to the room and intrude on the solitutde they now shared? He, pretending not to have noticed the switch; she, looking at him, still loving him, thinking thoughts that she would never say to Beverly. Or perhaps to anyone.

Sometimes, Beverly noticed Adele's lips moving as she walked around campus alone. She was talking to herself. Beverly wondered what she was saying.

What manner of words were these that were so powerful that they forced the lips to move, but so unspeakable that they caused the voice to retreat? Only the eyes, when caught off guard and locked in an involuntary embrace, could not feign muteness.

Suddenly, Beverly heard footsteps approaching slowly, cautiously. Her head felt heavy and she could barely move it to look in the direction of the halting, shy footsteps. Out of the corner of her eye, she glimpsed Adele's sandaled feet, finding a resting place beside her.

Beverly looked up at Adele. Her face was blank, but her eyes betrayed an uneasiness that Beverly sought to quell. So she let her eyes, soft and moist, speak for her. She steadied them on Adele's eyes until she could feel Adele's heartbeat calm.

Slowly, Beverly extended her right hand up toward Adele. "Why can't we be friends?" she whispered.

Adele thought she heard Beverly speak to her, but the question was asked so softly that she wasn't sure if Beverly had spoken it, or if she herself had simply thought it. She had taken to talking to herself lately, and sometimes it was hard for her to distinguish the whispers of other women from the whispers of her own soul.

But Beverly's hand was extended toward her, so it must have been Beverly's voice that she'd heard seconds before.

Hesitantly, Adele grasped Beverly's hand, almost businesslike. She didn't mean for it to be so formal, but she could tell by the hurt look that crossed Beverly's eyes—for less than a second—that her hand was cold, limp.

But Beverly quickly got over it. She held Adele's hand in both of hers for a long moment. She could feel Adele's hand warming up as it nestled reluctantly in the fold that Beverly had created for it. Slowly, Beverly brought Adele's hand to her lips. Gently, she kissed Adele's hot hand.

Suddenly, Beverly heard footsteps approaching slowly, cautiously. Her head felt heavy and she could barely move it to look in the direction of the halting, shy footsteps. Out of the corner of her eye, she glimpsed Adele's sandaled feet.

Wait a minute. She had been dreaming. Daydreaming under the nighttime sky. She and Adele hadn't crossed any great divides after all, except in Beverly's own optimistic head.

But here was a chance to make it real.

Beverly looked up at Adele. Her face was blank, but her eyes betrayed an uneasiness that Beverly wanted to quell.

Adele would have none of it. As if spurred by what she saw in Beverly's face, Adele hurriedly picked up her feet from their resting place beside Beverly and walked away.

Beverly was stunned by the abruptness of it all. But she was rarely speechless.

"See you later," Beverly called out to Adele, disappointment edging her voice.

" Bye," Adele said from a distance.

Beverly listened to Adele's fading footsteps.▲

Bridgett M. Davis is an assistant professor at Baruch College (CUNY) in Manhattan, where she teaches journalism and literature. A native of Detroit, Ms. Davis attended Spelman College and Columbia University. She has had brief stints as a reporter for newspapers in Atlanta and Philadelphia and now writes about black artists for various publications. She is a contributing author to *The Black Women's Health Book*.

Bianca is excerpted from Ms. Davis' first novel, entitled *Nights Without Color*.

"For me, life is essentially a sensual experience," says Ms. Davis. "And I try through my writing to recreate that effect, to enable readers to come away from my work satisfied that they've fully engaged their senses. And if they discover later that their intellect and spirit were somehow permeated too, that's all the better."

Ms. Davis, who lives in Fort Greene, Brooklyn with her Yorkshire Terrier, Magick, is currently working on a screenplay about black women artists.▲

BIANCA

by BRIDGETT M. DAVIS

Bianca slowly pushes a needle into her black chenille sweater, then pulls it through, arcing her arm high above as the heavy black thread follows. Tiny gold sequins cling feebly to the sweater, waiting to be sewn back in place. They jiggle, then sparkle in the dim light of her little room. She pauses to puff her cigarette.

Nighttime is easing atop the daylight. In two hours, Bianca will be singing at the Nuits Blanches Club. She isn't ready. Her throat feels rough, scratchy, rebellious. She wishes she had honey and lemon to sip, to soothe. *I talked too much today in French class,* she thinks. *All that silliness about Thomas and his car. "Thomas, votre voiture est tres rapide, n'est pas?" Who cares? Who ever asks men named Thomas if their cars are fast? French classes should teach practical phrases, like, Of course it's yours. There's been no one else.*

This thought tickles Bianca and she laughs, causing the sweater in her lap to shake as two glittery sequins float to the floor, twirling and twirling before they land. The sight of their slow-motion fall makes her angry, robs the moment of its humor.

"Shit!" she says, tossing the sweater aside. Bianca rises, stands before the long mirror nailed to the closet door. She poses, bare chest brazen, hands on her hips. She picks up her sweater, slips it on over black stretch pants and pulls two sequins off the right flower design to match the one on the left. She likes this sweater, a real find at a vintage shop in L.A. She enjoys wearing a garment with some stranger's past woven in its cloth. She reaches for her cigarette, puffs hard, stubs it out in an I LOVE NEW YORK ashtray. She doesn't love New York. She loves Paris.

She has loved Paris since she visited the city for a week's vacation two years ago. One look at the Eiffel Tower jutting into the skyline and she was determined to save her money, sell her few possessions and move to the City of Lights. Her goal was to be aboard an airplane, en route to France, on her birthday. She made it.

This is good, she thinks, studying herself in the mirror.

Strong, dark, 30-year-old face . . .

She was never cute. Her eyes are set far apart, her lips big and her long, slightly tilted nose out of sync with her face. Growing up, boys chose her to play first base, saved their love taps for the other, smaller, delicate-faced girls. She never learned that a flutter of the eyelashes or a coy glance could lure the opposite sex. Unaware, she courted herself instead of men.

Long fingers, square dignified hands . . .

Her mother had wanted her to learn the piano with those long fingers, but her father had taught her to garden instead. He'd been a landscaper for rich people living along the Florida Keys. By the time Bianca was 10, he was 65 and retired. She helped him cultivate the little gardens on his own two-acre property. In silence, they would plant, weed and prune rows and rows of vegetables in one plot, flowers in another. Her father didn't talk much. He let her wear overalls, taught her how to plant seeds beneath a full moon and water them at dawn, making the earth damp and ready for the sun. She used to imitate him, cracking her knuckles, then pulling the fingers until the joint popped—creating a pair of female hands still long, yet big-boned and strong.

Short, sculpted afro . . .

She doesn't like her hair when it grows longer than this, gets independent of her. Bianca spent seven years as a hairdresser once, in her other life. She worked her way through perky salons where circular light bulbs blazed around mirrors and everyone called everyone else Babe. Her clients were all white women. She loved their hair, thin and silky like horse tails or full and cottony like French Poodles. Washed in two minutes, blown dry in five. Straight-forward, honest hair. Easy work. Nothing like the hair salon—beauty parlor—in St. Petersburg, Florida where her mother stood on her feet, working for 10 hours a day for 20 years. Where permanent callouses grew on her mother's index and middle fingers from years of clicking smooth, blue-handled hot curlers between them. Sometimes burning her forefinger as she placed a hot pressing comb against a young girl's scalp.

The smell Bianca hated most. Hair frying. Cooked like catfish in melted grease or burned like a wayward lover in pungent lye. Hot curlers, hot dryers and hot combs used to whip those women's hair into shape, into submission.

"Sit still Beatrice," her mother would say whenever she sat her down in that salon chair and came after her with the straightening comb. Her mother was business-like, curt and impatient with her, wasting no jokes or easy conversation on Beatrice the way she did paying customers. Fast was her mother, efficient and merciless—pulling the child's coarse hair back in a marble-topped rubber band so tight the neighborhood children called her Chinese Eyes.

She stopped sitting in her mother's parlor chair on a Tuesday when she was 14. That was the day her mother swung her around in that swivel seat and made her look at herself in the stark, bulb-less mirror.

"There's some things a girl ought to know about herself," said her mother, eyes staring hard into the reflection of Beatrice's smooth face. "You just listen to what I got to say. Don't you say nothing 'til I'm through."

Her mother parted a section of her hair, combed it, oiled it, sliced a hot come through it, making it sizzle. Then she slipped the curlers with blue handles into their open-ended oven, leaned back, took a breath.

"Your daddy, he's not really your daddy."

Beatrice didn't move, didn't blink. Her mother kept clicking, clicking, clicking the curlers giving her daughter Shirley Temple curls she was already too old to believe in.

"It was just something that happened, before I found the Lord. I don't want you fretting over it. Your daddy, he don't know, praise the Lord. But you, you're a young woman now and you need this here information to keep you clear on who you are. No need for somebody out there in the streets to think they can tell you more about yourself than you can."

Beatrice stared back unblinking at her mother's reflection. "That's not true."

"Look at yourself." Her mother nodded her head at the mirrored reflection. "Do you look like him?"

"My nose," she said, touching a nostril with the tip of her finger. "Daddy always said I had his nose. He always told me that."

Her mother shook her head. "I did that, gave you that there nose. Do you know what hell this here household woulda been in if you'da come out with a pug nose? Praise the Lord! Lowery Jr., that was your real Daddy's name, he's dead now. Now he had him a broad, wide nose. And I could see right off, you was gonna have my color, my eyes and his nose. So I rubbed it long. From the time you was a baby, I rubbed it every night. Sometimes before you fell asleep, sometimes after. Molding things on a baby is easy to do, what with their bones still soft-like and changeable. Why, Bruce Walker's got two little dents in his head today because his daddy gripped onto him the wrong way when he was a baby. Praise the Lord."

Her mother dipped one finger into a can of Royal Crown pomade, rubbed the grease between her hands, then smoothed it on her daughter's hair, pressing down so it made Beatrice's head go back, chin cutting the air and lumpy throat facing the ceiling. Finally, the mother placed a rough, greased palm against each of Beatrice's soft cheeks and whispered to the mirror. "Child, don't think too much on it. Talked it over with your Aunt Ethel and she agreed with me. Figured life would be easier for you all the way round with a nice, long nose. Just thank me, thank God and go on 'bout your business. The Bible say, 'My God will supply all your needs according to his riches in glory by Christ Jesus.' Praise the Lord." Then her mother patted Beatrice's shoulder three times, the way she did her customers before she said, "That'll be six dollars. You have a good day now. Keep that hair oiled and I'll see you in two weeks."

That was a long time ago. The last time she sat in her mother's parlor chair. She was relieved when the Black Power movement came to Florida, freeing her from her mother's hostile hot comb. She wore an afro, big and bushy at first. As she grew older, the hair got shorter. She kept it natural and it kept her free. Free like the white girls. Free to walk into the shower with shampoo instead of a shower cap and free to go swimming without concerns about her hair going back.

At 16, Beatrice left home. She took nothing with her, not even her name. Left it in the beauty parlor mirror, in her mother's creased face, in those rough hands that had rubbed her father away.

She ran off to a university in Arizona, the one that sent a nice letter to the house saying they were looking for Negro girls to train to be nurses. That didn't last. She attended two classes, then never returned. The maxim "Doctor Knows Best" irritated her. She decided to do hair instead. What Phoenix did teach Bianca was the sex appeal of a sunrise. For the ten months she lived there, enrolled in beauty school, she often stayed up through the night—forgetting to sleep just to watch the way the sun slipped out of the flat earth, rich and orange and runny as an egg yolk naked from its shell. But a sunrise isn't everything.

Her next stop had been Atlanta. "Southern comfort is what I know," she told a manicurist friend the night before she left Arizona.

Then came New York. "The Big Apple has so many people, nobody will have time to pay me any attention," she said to Joel, her Georgian roommate. "You can have my bicycle. I won't be needing it."

Los Angeles was next. She liked L.A.: Working at a salon in Beverly Hills, catching famous and beautiful women with water dripping down their faces, shampoo stinging their eyes. Still, flawless women can be boring too.

"I don't think I could live in another country, always feeling like an outsider," said her Californian girlfriend, Wendy, as she helped Bianca pack for her move to France.

"Paris is the only place I feel like an insider," Bianca said, rolling a pair of leggings and stuffing them into the corner of her khaki duffel bag. "It's like finding your soul mate. I just know I'll fit in there."

"Yeah, maybe. But I've seen those movies about American expatriates who never really feel accepted" Wendy frowned. "You know, they're not French, so they get snubbed, then they come back here and they don't feel right in America because they've been gone too long. They don't fit in *anywhere*. I mean, look at poor Rick in *Casablanca*. That's no real life, if you ask me."

"You watch too many movies, Wendy. Besides, I'm not going to be an ex-whatever-the-word-is. I'm finally going to belong somewhere, live someplace that feels like home for a change."

"You'll get bored, Bianca. You're a drifter. Face it. Wherever you lay your hat is your home."

"So I'm laying my hat in Paris, okay? Now, help me zip up this bag, honey, before I miss my plane."

****

Now she is here. Singing. A year she has been in Paris, first washing the hair of French women in a salon near the Champs-Elysées. Traveling across the border to Amsterdam every two months to renew her visitor's stamp in her passport. Shocking the salon owner when he asked her to do the hair of the models from Martinique, Ivory Coast and Haiti who came in for quick wash, blow dry and curls. "I don't know how to do black women's hair," she told him. He fired her right then, said "he needed a more versatile American girl working for him."

"Ahhh, your voice, it's so, how do you say, sultry." The French men said that to her. They found her voice husky, its masculine sound making it ever more arresting and inviting.

"You are a singer, no?" They asked that question again and again. One day she walked into a tiny bistro near Montparnasse and announced: "Je suis une chanteuse. I am a singer." They hired her.

Now she is a singer—with Rolland's band. Rolland knows she grew up listening to no music in her mother's strict, Pentacostal house. Nothing except an Aretha Franklin album slipped to her by a next-door neighbor. She played it very low on a record player she kept hidden under her bed. She'd have to lie on the floor to listen. To Bianca, the gospel-tinged soul singer sounded like what music magazines said she was—a "fast" preacher's daughter. In the world and of it. Bianca thought of her as a kindred spirit. So that, the day she decided to start singing, she had only Aretha as a guide. Not to sound like her, but to sing like her—without faking. So Bianca opened her mouth and let whatever come out, to hear what her own life sounded like. Every time she sang, she was as eager as the audience to discover what that sound was. Based on how one phrase came out, she'd adjust the next. So Bianca seldom sang the same way twice. In fact, she didn't think of it as singing. She thought of it as exploring herself while people watched. It excited her.

"The most erotic place in the world to be," she told Rolland, "is on stage. I mean, where else?"

Bianca wants a residence permit. She needs a permanent job, which means she needs Rolland. Or she needs citizenship, which means she needs a husband. A husband who will be too full of himself to notice the absence of domestic detail. A husband who will give her a Yorkshire Terrier and a house. She'll give him foot massages and occasionally sex. Then Paris will truly be home.

*****

In the hall, she can hear the girls' laughter. They are waiting for her outside the door. They knock, two small fists with pink knuckles rapping in unison. Bianca swings open the door.

"We are so long waiting for you," says the long-haired, blonde one. They are French girls, sisters, young, gigly. Virginie and Magdeleine. They want Bianca to call them Ginnie and Maggie. "We will walk with you to the club," says Magdeleine, the short-haired brunette. Bianca hugs them both. The girls enjoy speaking English with her, to improve their own textbook knowledge of American talk. Bianca's fragmented French barely gets the same workout when she is with them.

She met them near the university. Magdeleine was carrying three books: one by Camus, another by Anaïs Nin and her own hardcover diary. Virginie's hands were free. They have become useful friends, these giggly girls. They usher Bianca through the real Paris, the Paris kept tucked away from tourists behind affected French snobbery. Bianca has sat in the window seat of their parents' summer chateau and secretly watched their *maman* crying on the lawn. She has slept overnight, three abreast in the giant, soft featherbed of the girls' sprawling apartment with its view of Notre-Dame. There they curl up on either side and feed her stories of quiet, French childhoods, of times when they brought home good grades from boarding school and their mother let them crawl into her bed and sleep beside her. "It is a very big treat for French children to sleep with their mamans," explained Magdeleine. "It is very much a honor."

And too, she has drunk champagne from crystal glasses while listening to the girls' uncle play French nursery rhymes on the grand piano while everyone drank too much and sang and laughed. The uncle Bianca thinks of often. His blue eyes smiling at her over the piano keys as he sings. He speaks little English. She speaks less French. They have seen each other twice. They smile across rooms.

*****

"Let's hurry, I want to get to the club early tonight," says Bianca, grabbing both girls' hands as they head out of her room at the student residence and onto the crowded streets of Boulevard St-Michel.

An American dance movie is playing at the St-Michel Cinema. Bianca stares into the eyes of the girl looming over them on the billboard above, her long legs gapped, a ripped t-shirt dropping from a shoulder blade. Bianca likes her. She read that this girl auditioned for the leading part in the movie without knowing how to dance. And she got the part. Someone else, someone unknown, someone with hair like hers filmed the dance scenes. But this girl, the one staring down from the billboard, got the part. "She's flawless," says Bianca as they pass under the Flashdancing girl's stare. "Flawless."

Ten blocks they walk to the club and once there, Jean Claude, the owner, jokes with her about her portable fan club. The French girls enjoy being groupies. They plop down at a front table, happy to sit for an hour before the show begins. Jean Claude prepares hot water and lemon for Bianca's throat. She carries the drink to the empty stage, stands spread eagle and sips.

"Mademoiselle, I have a message for you," says Jean Claude, approaching the stage. "It is a caller from London. A Jasmine Bridges. She has left for you a number." He hands her a piece of paper.

"Jasmine?" Bianca pauses. *Oh,* she thinks. *That doe-eyed girl who came dancing with us at Le Place a while ago. The one Rolland brings around the club sometimes.* Bianca stares at the paper in her hand. *What does she want with me? She wears skirts and high heels. She's one of them.*

For years, Bianca has stayed away from other black women. She believes they talk about black men as if their penises are jewel-encrusted. "My man this" and "My man that." And when they're not talking about their men and how to keep them, they're talking about other women.

"Girl, did you see what that child had on? Now you know she ain't had no business wearing a dress that tight. Must be a leftover from the old days when she was two sizes smaller."

She used to listen to them talking on and on in her mother's beauty parlor. She doesn't understand them, their conversations, their preoccupations. So obsessed with holding on to their lover-men. Lover-men with whom they eat big, home-cooked meals, only to go on crash diets. Lover-men with whom they sit lethargically in front of ball games they don't understand, only to frantically join aerobics classes later. Lover-men for whom they spend their money on silk dresses with matching pumps to show off big behinds and big legs, only to pay their rents ten days late. And lover-men for whom they get their hair fixed on Saturday mornings, only to sweat out the edges in Saturday night beds. She doesn't understand them.

The only black women she ever knew were the ones who came through her mother's shop and the ones who went to school with her at St. Petersburg Grammar and High. They were all the same. You mention the way the sun comes up over the horizon at dawn and makes the dew glisten on magnolia leaves, they want to tell you how white women are taking their men. As if that somehow changes the beauty of a sunrise. Black women, she thinks, don't notice the blues and oranges and greens of the world. They know only two colors. Absorbing life the way her mother watched the *Wizard of Oz*—on the old black & white TV. By the time she and Toto landed in Oz, for all Bianca's mother knew, Dorothy hadn't gone anywhere. She was still in Kansas.

Here in Paris, Bianca can experience every color Oz has to offer. She can meet people, people who accept her and can help her. People like the French girls. The giggly sisters are fascinated by her, without judgment and without expectation. They could never say, "Who she think she is, Miss Thing, walking around like she don't recognize the black on her?" the way girls whispered when she walked by back in St. Petersburg.

She wants to get to know the French girls' uncle. He could be the answer to her residency dilemna. Or Rolland. He could help too. She thinks of this as she walks into Jean Claude's office, closes the door, grabs his private telephone and dials the London number.

"Hello?" says Jasmine.

"It's Bianca honey. I heard you called?"

"Yes . . . yes I did," says Jasmine. Her voice is breathy. "I'll be in Paris for the day. To shop. And, well, I wanted to talk to you about . . . I have a favor to ask of you. I wanted to know if you'd have time to meet me for lunch tomorrow?"

"A favor?" Bianca raises her eyebrows. "You want a favor from me?"

"Yes I do. But I have to talk to you about it in person, okay?"

"Alright, I suppose we could meet. If you like."

Jasmine lets go of a fat sigh. "Good. Is noon all right?"

"Fine. You could meet me here at the club." Bianca says goodbye, then shakes her head.

Why would she want a favor from me? she thinks. *"I don't have anything she could use."*

The soft strains of Rolland's sax drift back into the office. Bianca clears her throat, then strolls quickly out the room, moving toward another night of what she's come to crave—anonymous applause. ▲

Trey Ellis was born in 1962 in Washington, DC. After graduating from Stanford University he completed his critically acclaimed first novel, *Platitudes* (Vintage Contemporaries). His second novel is *Home Repairs* (Simon & Schuster). He is also the author of the essay, "The New Black Aesthetic" and numerous articles for *The Village Voice, Callaloo, Newsweek* and *Interview*. In his spare time, Trey writes screenplays for the monster that is Hollywood.▲

GUESS WHO'S COMING TO SEDER

by TREY ELLIS

What?
SHHHHH.

So now you, my son, my only son, shush me? The one who took all your vicious kicks. Like a Nazi bastard you goose-stepped in my belly and now with the shush?

BUBA.

So now with the Yiddish? I thought you'd forgotten in front of your pretty shiksa wife and your goyim friends, call me Mammy or something?

Mrs. Cohen's son, Alan, explodes his eyes overwide at his mother's bifocal lenses. Hidden absolutely are her eyes, instead, the weighty glasses only televise the two candle flames next to the two platefulls of matzah in front of her.

It's getting late. Alan. Megan. Donnel Washington eyes first his wife Carlene, then Vietta, his little girl. Their six palms push on the tablecloth, raising their asses off the cane geometry of the Cohens' chairs' seat bottoms simultaneously.

Donnel, please. My mother's from New York and she's lost almost all her hearing and her mind too. She doesn't mean anything by it. Carlene, I'm sorry.

You call *this* wine? Does *she* think French is kosher now that she's an expert on our religion or something?

Heather, *please* pass your grandmother the Mogan David. Megan Cohen, Heather's mother, starts to throw her hands at her mother-in-law's trachea but snatches them back to wring her own blonde bun.

Heather slides the now wet curl of brown hair from the soft crack between her lips, latches it behind an ear. Pouring, her right nipple, through her bra and her blouse, jostles a liver spot on her grandmother's bare triceps. The noise of a car's wheels rolling, its engine screwing through missed gears to stop near the house, pulls Heather's eyes, her head to the door.

Such large, firm roses. I had such firm roses when I was young and sweet too, back when grandfather was alive . . . but what use are they to anyone now that they hang over the fat of my belly like dead things. Heatherchick, if you go a day in your life without wearing a brassiere, so help me God I'll chop yours off.

Drink the first cup of wine, and fill Elijah's cup. Pass around a basin to wash the hands. Take parsley or spring onion, dip them in vinegar or salt water, pass them around the table, and say:
"Blessed are you YHWH our God, Ruler of the Universe who create the fruit of the earth."
"Barukh atay YHWH elohenu melekh ha-olam boray p'ri ha a-da-mah."

It's a shame Derrick isn't here for this part of the ceremony. I think he would have liked it. Heather, you're sure you told him eight o'clock?

Yes, Dad. I told you already he has a big paper due. But I don't know where he is *all* the time. You *could* ask Mister and Miz Washington.

Carlene and Donnel Washington smile with Alan and Megan Cohen at the new pink on Heather's face.

We must apologize for him. I left a note on the kitchen table, but that boy's so willful no telling what mess he's into now. As she speaks about her son, Carlene reties the bow that her daughter has again untied in the burnt offering of her hot-combed hair.

Mah nishtanah ha-lai-lah? Mah nishtanah ha-lai-lah? Who's going to say it already? Billy, you're the baby, so tell me what is it that holds you so quiet?

Billy Cohen slurps the dangling lunger of saliva back through his lips but not before the last inch and three-quarters detaches, dives through the red surface of his Paschal wine, floats back white bubbles.

ACTUALLY BUBA, VIETTA WASHINGTON IS THE YOUNGEST. Vietta, could you please read from the top of page 72. Where it says, Why is this night . . .

Vietta looks hard at her mother. Ma, can't I just eat the crackers? I feel stupid.

Go on, baby. Don't be bashful. Carlene pets her neck.

Let Derrick do it, if he ever makes it. This is all his fault anyway.

Don't make me tell you twice.

[Huff] "Whyisthisnightdifferentfromallothernights? On all, other, nights we may—"

What? I'm sure she's not speaking Hebrew. Then let me help for God's sake: She-b'khol ha-le-lot a-nu okh-lin sh'ar y'ra-kot, ha-lai-lah ha-zeh ma-ror. She-b'khol ha-le-lot eyn anu mat-bilin a-fi-lu p-am a-chat, ha-lai-lah ha-zeh sh-tay f'a-mim. She-b'khol ha-le-lot a-nu okh-lin beyn yosh-vin u-veyn m'su-bin, ha-lai-lah ha-zeh ku-la-nu m'su-bin.

THANK YOU, BUBA. Continue reading, Vietta, please?

The teaching invites us to meet and to teach four children: one wise and one wicked, one innocent and one who does not relate by asking.
What does the wise one say? "What are the testimonies, and the statues, and the rules whic . . . ?"

. . . which Y-H-W . . . ?

Yahweh, Vietta. It's a sin for Jews to pronounce the real name of Him or Her.

You mean you can't say GOD-GOD-GOD-GOD-GOD!

I'll slap the black off you, girl, when we get home. Apologize.

That's OK, Carlene, my mother started it. Alan's eyes flick to their corners to watch his mother.

So now with the killer looks? At your own mother even? I wish I could've heard what terrible things you've all been spitting at me now that I'm deaf, more dead than alive, my last seder in all probability.

Invite and wait for discussion on these questions:
Who are the four children? Are they among us? Are they within each of us?
Are these good answers?

It must be time to talk about the four children now and of course they are still with us, especially the wicked one who's lost the language, doesn't even get bat mitzvahed like my beautiful granddaughter next to me, or who marries out of the religion like my only son, so technically my two grandchildren here aren't even really Jewish. Back in olden times these would have been the ones saying, Freedom, shmeedom, I'd rather stay here with this bunch of greasy Arabs as their dirty slave . . . no offense.

Carlene crinkles the skin around her eyes, raising weakly her cheeks and upper lip from her teeth.

WHY SHOULD ANYONE BE OFFENDED, BUBA? All of us, blacks and Jews, have been enslaved, there's no hiding from it, right?

Come on, Alan, *our* emancipation was a tad more recent, don't you think? Were your great-grandparents born slaves? Hmmm? The knife in Donnel's left hand, coated in haroseth (ritualized mortar made of diced apples and nuts, wine and raisins), disintegrates the matzah (representing the brick), in his right hand. Haroseth and matzah flakes stucco his palm then the napkin.

Yes, but . . . Heather honey, what's your take on all this?

I don't know.

Come on now, sweetie, is tonight really that bad?

Heather handles the bottle of kosher French by its neck, jams its nose into the bottom of her glass until the rising choppy waves of wine redden her knuckles, then overflow and wound the white tablecloth.

Heatherchick! You know that it's not yet that we toast. I swear before your grandfather's ghost you even *sip* before the right time and PING! there again goes my blood clot and half of my face will die like your Aunt Estelle's in the home.

Lifting the glass to her mouth, Heather looks at no one. Noisily, gulp after gulp of wine bubbles back around her mouth's corners.

Young lady, that wasn't too nice. Megan turns a bit from her daughter, tilts her face into her hand, milks her rising smile from her cheeks into her palm.

Mrs. Cohen whistles "Dai Dai Eun" at the Hockney lithograph on the wall.

BUBA, WE'RE STILL TRYING TO DISCUSS THE FOUR

CHILDREN AS THE B'NAI B'RAK RABBI'S INSTRUCTED.

Now it's getting very late Megan, Alan, and Vietta have school tomorrow.

So they're leaving in the middle of seder? They hate Jewish so that they want calamity to strike us all down?

Uh, Donnel, I'm so sorry. My mother thinks if anyone leaves, gets up from their chair before the last cup of wine is drunk, all the Jews in the house will be slain. See, in 1583, there was this thing in Istanbul.

Maybe they're Farrakhan mooslims.

I'll have you know that the Washingtons' son, Derrick, and our Megan, have been seeing each other all through U of M, so they might very soon be *family.*

Ma!

After discussion, all sing.
Go tell it on the mountain,
over the hills and everywhere.
Go tell it on the mountain—
Let my people go!
Who are the people dressed in white?
Let my people go!
Must be the children of the Israelite—
Let my people go!

Where did you get this hippie seder from anyhow?

Cousin Naomi found it at the Rainbow Reformed Temple in New York.

[A moment of silence. Then a reader says:]
"But let us also question the plagues: Can the winning of freedom be bloodless? It was not bloodless when Nat Turner proclaimed, I had a vision, and I saw white spirits and black spirits engaged in battle, and the sun was darkened—the thunder rolled in the heavens and blood flowed in streams—and I heard a voice saying, Such is your luck, such you are called to see, and let it come rough or smooth, you must surely bear it.'"
I-lu i-lu ho-tzi-a-nu, ho-tzi-a-nu mi-mitz-ra-yim, ho-tzi-a-nu- mi-mitz-ra-yim dai-ye-nu. DAI-DAI-YE-NU, DAI-DAI-YE-NU, DAI-DAI-YE-NU, dayenu, dayenu!
[All drink the third cup. Refill glasses, but not to the top.]
     [The door is opened]

Alan returns Vietta's bow from the floor to her lap, slouches down to her as she confetties her paper napkin. It's almost over, sweetheart, then Billy can show you his Nintendo. He just got Donkey Kong. We're just waiting a little bit for the ghost of Elijah to come down and drink his cup of wine. If you leave milk and cookies out for Santa Clause, it's sort of like that. Alan stretches to pat Vietta's shoulder but she flinches.

Miss Thing, I raised you better than acting up like this outside the house.

Dingdingding-Dong.

Billy's curtains of matzah-flaked lips pull back, reveal teeth behind braces. Heather's back straightens, red reclaims her face.

Did I hear the doorbell go off? At least this you did right, my little Alan. Mrs. Cohen laughs. The messiah rings the doorbell! My uncle's half-brother, Arkady, the Shostakovich of indoor plumbing, used to rig a pump to Elijah's cup to make it look like the spirit was drinking it. Oh how I always fell for that as a girl.

Dingdingding-Dong.

Heather, get the door, it's okay.

I miss any good fights? Sorry I'm late. I had to . . . finish a paper. Derrick shrugs out of his jean jacket, flies it to the coat rack. He peels off the black beret, jiggles the tiny dreadlocks on his head's top re-erect.

Of one thing I'm sure, the Messiah, this is not.

Shut up, mother.

What?

Derrick, you knew how much this meant to Heather. Your mother and I are very disappointed in you . . . . We'll talk about this at home. Go take your seat.

You're just in time to read, Derrick.

Uh, sorry, Mr. Cohen, but my eyes are watering so much from reading all day at the libr—His mother's eyes freeze his tongue.

Brothers and sisters, we have been remembering our slavery and our liberation. But just as it was we, not our forbearers only, who were liberated in Egypt, so it is we, not our forebearers only, who live in slavery. The task of liberation is long and it is work that we ourselves must do.

> *[All sing]*
> *We shall overcome,*
> *We shall overcome,*
> *We shall overcome some day!*
> *Deep in my heart, I do believe,*
> *We shall overcome some day.*
> *We'll walk hand in hand . . . (Repeat as "We shall overcome")*
> *We are not afraid . . . (Repeat . . .)*
> *The people shall be free . . . (Repeat . . .)*
> *Black and white together . . . (Repeat . . .)*
> *We shall live in peace . . . (Repeat . . .)*

We shall overcome!
[Dance Joyfully]

Now can I go play Donkey Kong? Please?▲

Tamara Jeffries, 27, makes her living as an editor and writer in Atlanta. A native of Danville, VA, she earned a journalism degree from Hampton University, and has worked at newspapers, a magazine company, and a marketing firm. Her first published short story, "Little Anderson," won the *Essence* 1991 short story contest. She is currently working on a collection of short fiction, and is trying to find time to research a socio-historical novel.

I've made my living writing and editing since I left college, but when anyone asked me what I did, I'd tell them I worked for a newspaper or worked for a magazine or whatever. I never called myself a writer. That was for the folks who were freelancing or producing fiction. Now I still have a "day job," but I also get up every morning and put some words down—for me. I'm pulling ideas together, rewriting, revising, and sending out manuscripts. Now, when people ask me what I do, I say, "I'm a writer." And I have to smile; it still feels strange—good strange.

I want to tell stories that reveal unusual relationships and honor the invisible people—people who don't think they have anything to say or who don't think anyone cares. I like the challenge of trying to get inside some character's head, and then writing about what's in there.

It's important for our people to have voices and to be able to express themselves. Too many of us who are creative and expressive don't know how to give that a form. I guess, eventually, I'll be standing in front of a classroom trying to tell people how to do that in writing. Both my parents are teachers; several of my aunts taught and my sister is a teacher. It's in my genes.▲

ORPHAN

by TAMARA JEFFRIES

Fuck this! Fuck this shit!" Reg's anger, pitched high, shattered the concentrated silence. "What *is* this shit, man? What are we *doing* here?"

It was Sunday evening. We—the two of us and a couple of draftsmen—were in the office trying to get a project ready for a presentation. The Big Picture Boys had been in for a minute, overseen, and left us to take care of the details. They trusted our work. (With good reason.) Our reward was that we got to spend our weekends hunched over our drafting tables.

"We been here all day today, all day yesterday. All fucking week til 11, 12, 1 o'clock in the morning, scrambling like lab rats to finish a design for another goddamn, hermetically sealed, high-security building just like this one. I am *sick* of this *bullshit*." He pounded brutally, straining the delicate joints of his drafting table. Pencils and pens scattered, paper curled out of his way, and a near-empty Chinese carton sputtered cold fried rice. Sticky brown liquid from a wounded Coke can trickled along the fine blue lines that indicated a carefully engineered skybridge; the draftsmen winced but didn't move.

"It's Sunday, man. Sunday. My grandaddy had to work *three* jobs just to put food on the table, but *he* drew the line at working on Sunday."

"Your grandaddy wasn't on salary," I said, sort of under my breath, trying to cool him out.

"Naw." He whispered, quiet and hot like cigarette smoke, into my face. "Nah, my grandaddy wasn't on fucking salary."

"Hold up, man, it was just a joke. I was just . . . ."

"Nah, man, you're right." Hands up, under arrest, he turned away to stare blindly across the city skyline. "He wasn't on salary. Shit, he wasn't on hourly. He had to take whatever they gave him. And he took it. Trying to feed seven kids and send them to school somewhere so they wouldn't have to work like dogs—like him. And look at me. Two generations later: a mothafucking sharecropper in a thousand dollar suit."

His voice fogged the plate-glass view; his eyes seemed dark, looking back inside his own head. He was really losing it.

"Hey, man look. Let's get outta here for a few, okay?" I eased him toward the door. "You're right: We been in here for damn near three days straight. Let's go get some real food, a drink, chill out for a minute. We need to get out." I motioned to the other guys that everything was cool; we'd be back. They just sat there, silent, watching. In the back of my mind, I played back this story the way it would sound when they reported it to the partners Monday morning.

When we got to the street, we started walking—out of the cavern of glass and granite buildings, toward the rubble of the warehouse district, neither of us saying anything.

I was trying to remember if I'd ever seen him this angry before—or mad at all. But Reg was always in control—crisp, cool, starched, dry. Always. The maddest I'd ever seen him was when, after he refused to give up a quarter, some panhandling brother spit on the Italian wool Zegna suit he'd almost finished paying for. His neck tightened in his starched collar and it seemed like a long time before he unlocked his eyes from the guy's face, but he just moved away without saying anything—then or later.

At the office, they didn't know *how* to take him. He was direct, smart as hell, very talented. He managed to tightrope that fine line between cocky and confident, friendly and fuck you. And his total, unswerving cool totally unnerved them. They watched him, waiting for him to slip up. I watched them try to figure out why he never did. I wondered what their reaction would have been if they'd seen him tonight.

We ended up at Blue's, an upscale hole-in-the-wall where the so-called downtown buppies went for happy hour. It was nearly empty now, but remnants of weekend cigarettes and cognac curtained the room. Reg slid tight in the corner of a booth, his face shadowed, until the waitress came with his E&J. Then he pushed himself forward continuing the story he'd obviously been narrating in his head. I hadn't heard the beginning, but I knew the plot. It was the same story, really, that all of us had. A collective biography.

". . . I remember standing in front of the bus station the day I left for college. Mama was wiping tears, leaving little bits of tissue on her face. Pops just clamped onto my shoulder, looked me in the eye and said, 'Don't forget.' The night before he had come in my room and sat down in the middle of all my junk, and started telling me the story about his grandfather and great-grandfather and his daddy—how they had worked and fought and saved to get something to pass on, so the next generation could live a little better. I'd heard the story before. A thousand times. But this time he looked at me and said 'That was for you, son. They didn't know it, I guess, but all that struggling was for this day. Don't you forget that.' Just like that, he laid generations worth of laboring and crying and fighting and dying all right on my back. And I've been carrying it with me ever since."

It was freight we all carried, inherited from parents and grandparents and their parents. We shouldered it, along with images of the passers-on; slaves and sharecroppers with backs numbed from bending; factory workers double-shifting on tired feet; and the maids, the cooks, the yardmen, the washerwomen with tongues bitten to bleeding to mask the endless indignations. Our parents had marched during The Movement, but they were weary when the news finally came from the mountain top, so they passed the legacy of striving on to us, and told us to crossover.

They told us we could do anything we set our minds to if we worked hard and didn't mess up. And we did everything right just like the white boys. We educated ourselves meticulously. We learned how to talk properly. How to mimic their accents, their inflections, their slang. We dropped the big-ball games we had played in the 'hoods, and learned to play tennis and racquetball and golf. We quoted the *Journal.* We knew what was on the *Times Bestseller List.* We joined health clubs, saw the right films, made reservations at the right restaurants. Our wives had credentials we could recite proudly and we used our dual incomes to purchase homes in zip codes where notices for pre-approved credit cards appeared with satisfying regularity in the mail.

It was a science: We learned their ways and we copied them. To the letter, if we were cool; to absurd extremes, if we weren't.

"We can do everything they can, can't we man? Except *be* them. Now that's the catch, ain't it. 'Cause if you ain't one of them, nothing you do really matters. Not *what* you know, not *who* you know, not how you act." Reg's hollow laugh turned to a growl in his glass. "We keep telling each other, 'You have to work twice as hard to get half as far.' That's some of *their* shit, man. Some bullshit they made up to keep us on the run."

It was no different now than it had always been: We watched our backs and did their work; they looked past us and expected us to keep doing it. Now, eyes on the prize, we kept playing by their rules. But whatever we did was never enough. When we got up to speed, they shifted into another gear. When we learned their tricks, they changed them. They kept us interested by making empty promises: "You've got potential. A few more years. We've got our eyes on you."

And so did everyone else: Frat brothers, tennis partners, colleagues— waiting for you to break the tape or break down. Or the folks at home who had put you on a pedestal and held you there by the force of their expectation. They kept us at it with long-distance assurances and reminders of how proud they were; wishing grandmama could have seen you. But they didn't really understand. Retiring on slip-covered couches, they couldn't relate to our city-striving lives. They could brag discreetly about the fine jobs we had, but they couldn't really explain to their Elks brothers and mission board members what we actually did. So the homefolks would understand, marketing mangers, city editors, packaging engineers, and commodities brokers used the most simplistic explanations of their work—and thus reduced the impressive complexity of their occupations. And we couldn't make them understand why, with all the things we were able to acquire we still weren't satisfied. We didn't want to burst their proud bubbles—or ours—so we just talked to them less and less.

Reg was quiet for a moment as the waitress returned to replace our drained glasses with cool, strong drinks.

"And for all this, man, what have we got? Nothing. It all looks good.

From where Mama'nem stand it looks like I've got everything. But I don't have what my parents wanted. Shit, I don't even have what they *had.*

His story trailed off, but we sat under its heaviness until it evaporated. He lifted his head, finally, and looked up—through me.

"What are we doing here, man?" He stood up, threw some money toward the soggy cocktail napkin under his empty glass and walked away.

I saw Reg the other day, standing on the corner where I came up out of the subway. He wore a loose robe, stiff with needlework from his neck to his waist; a strip of grimy city-dirt bordered his pants' hem. His locks were still only tickling at his ears, but they had already begun to get that sun-rusted look. At first, I didn't recognize him sitting behind the table full of oils and incense. Then I caught the eyes—they were still dark, looking inward.

He didn't say anything, just smiled—a slight, ironic twist of his mouth—as he stepped out from behind his stand and moved toward me. His embrace was long and fierce, and when I left him, rushing to make it to the office on time, the smoky fragrance of Egyptian Musk lingered in my thousand dollar suit.▲

Yolanda Joe Our top story: Authorities are warning people to be on the lookout for a new writer.

  She is 29-year-old Yolanda Joe.

  Born in Chicago, and raised by her grandparents, Joe was caught writing poetry at the age of seven.

  The writing spree continued through grade and high school where Joe declared she wanted to be a novelist and a journalist.

  Shocked parents and teachers, tried to discourage this outlandish behavior and put Joe on the straight and narrow road to law school.

  For awhile, there was reform. Joe received a scholarship to Yale and there were few if any incidents of writing during this four-year period.

  During a stint at the Columbia School of Journalism in 1985, Joe lapsed back into her life of writing.

  Later that year she hit CBS in Chicago, pulling a small job in radio news before moving up to television news writing.

  The loot from most of her writing was found on her apartment floor—except for a short story that turned up in an anthology of Chicago women writers and a novel, FALLING LEAVES OF IVY (Longmeadow Press).

  If you see Joe's work, Authorities are asking people to please read carefully.▲

A GATHERING OF SONS

by YOLANDA JOE

All the months of freak accidents, ambulances, hospital rooms, tubes and needles, diagnosis, surgery, paralysis, therapy, releases, beds by the window with no view, few visitors, frustration, demands to be put away, arguments, giving-in, more hospitals, pneumonia, feelings of rejections, and comas . . . . all this had squeezed down to a single twitch in his left eye.

Stan looked at his father in the hospital bed. His breathing could barely be heard. His torso was frail and hollow with nothing to offer. His hands were puffy and waxy like dime-store balloons.

Look at your hands Daddy! Stan took a small, tinted bottle out of his back pocket. He took a big swig and continued staring at his father's hard, flat hands as they pressed the soft, white sheets. The last time they were both in a hospital room was 25 years ago when Stan had broken his leg. Daddy's image and voice from then came to Stan through a void of alarm.

"Do you see these hands?" Daddy said.

His hands were thick with muscles and hard from sawing wood and laying pipe. The knuckles were sun-burnt orange and the rest of his hands were his normal color of sand.

Stan swallowed and squirmed nervously in the hospital bed and tried vainly to explain. "See, this is what happened Daddy. I jumped on the back of the truck to catch a ride with Bainey and them and fell off and broke my leg."

WHACK-WHACK! Daddy's hands cuffed Stan's ears as he lay in the hospital bed. The pulley over his head was swinging from the vibrations. Stan hooked it with his right elbow and blocked the slaps with his left elbow, "C'mon Daddy I'm sick and in the hospital!"

He stopped.

Stan peeped at Daddy from behind his blocking elbow. Daddy's chest was punching away at his work shirt and sweat from the bald spot in the top of his head was running down his nose. His hands were dangling at his sides and his small, wiry body was tilting to the left.

Stan slowly began lowering his elbow, hoping it was safe.

A rush of emotions hit Daddy and he sorrowfully lifted up his arms in a widening loop.

"Daddy!" Stan shouted his blocking elbow snapping back up in defense.

Daddy dropped his hands back down and shoved them into his pockets. "Do everything the nurses tell you boy! I'll be back to see you tomorrow."

"Oh-okay, Daddy," Stan said still hiding behind his elbow. As the door closed, he breathed a sigh of relief and dropped his arm. Suddenly, the door opened again. Blocking elbow up: "I said okay Daddy!"

"I said okay Daddy," Benny mimicked in a mousey whine as he walked into the room followed by Hank. "Man, put your elbow down!"

Stan, relieved, stared as his two big brothers. Both had inherited their father's wiry build. Benny, a junior too cool to be called Grady, had on a blue windbreaker with smudges of dirt on it. His hair was already thinning in front like their father's and the thick oil from the marcel pulled his hair back into a "V". Hank wore a tee-shirt and jeans and flat, black shoes. His big, brown eyes were filled with water and kindness: "Hey, you feeling okay little brother?"

"Aww, he's alright," Benny answered before Stan could. "You always babying everybody, Hank!" Benny pointed at Stan. "Man, I'm not taking you nowhere else with me, so don't ask hear? Of all the dumb things to do! I told you to look at the girl as in turn your head and glance—not to fall out the truck trying to see! I ought to knock your head off!"

"Aww, heck-naw!" Stan raised his fist to his older brother. "I'm not taking no more licks today. Man, Daddy already tried to knock me silly in this hospital bed."

"Yeah, well, it wasn't no picnic for me either in the house last night! Daddy popped me around good for letting you follow behind me and get hurt!"

"Yeah," Hank said easing to the foot of the bed, "Madear says the doctor called late last night just as Daddy got back from his fishing trip. The doctor said that leg of yours might not never work right again." Hank stared at the bleached toes sticking out of the cast and wondered if Stan could feel. "Mister Mateson saw the accident and told Daddy you could've gotten killed or paralyzed."

"Aww, that's some shit . . ." Stan mumbled worriedly. "Ouch! Stop pinching my toes man!"

"Just checkin' is all," Hank nodded, satisfied. "Yep, Madear was crying and Daddy had this funny look on his face."

Stan took another swig now, swallowed the memory, and licked his lips. "You were scared weren't you Daddy? That's why you slapped me, huh?"

Daddy's left eye twitched.

I was scared too. Stan delicately picked up his father's hands and gently began kneading them.

"Hey Stan," a voice from behind him called.

Stan dropped his father's hands just as Hank began walking into the hospital room.

"Anybody else come?" Hank asked.

"James-D been here and gone mad too!" Stan said looking at his brother. Now you got that bald spot right in front like Daddy too. Stan patted the top of his own head, thankful he was left out of that inheritance. He dropped the same hand to his protruding stomach, then looked back at his father, as if to say, You should see how I've been putting it on Daddy.

Hank stopped by the bedside and clutched the rail. He pushed out with his arms, then pulled himself back in. The muscles in his wrists ached. He looked at the person in the bed; a masterpiece of the familiar stretched and molded by illness into a bad replica of Daddy. It was then that Hank realized that his father was actually dying. Hank leaned down and kissed Daddy's shoulder—the only place above the covers where there were no tubes.

"Aww, come on Hank!" Stan said in a whine. "Always kissing on folks. Get a hold of yourself!"

"I can kiss my father if I want to," Hank said not taking his eyes off that place on his shoulder. He saw a tear drying there.

"I've got to go to work. I'll see you later."

Hank looked back up at his brother. Stan's suit jacket was tight around the shoulders and arms. His hair was sandy brown and his face was huge and fair. Hank could smell a sweet mixture of expensive aftershave and Crown Royal whiskey. He longed for a drink too but dared not ask because he was supposed to be on the wagon. Hank watched as Stan left the room.

"Daddy, I'm sorry I haven't been coming to visit but the hospital's so far out and things at home just aren't right," Hank said softly. He pushed out on the railing. "I don't know how you took care of us all—a wife and seven sons—I just can't do it!" Always tried to be like you Daddy. Always have. His wrists curled and he pulled himself back in. "It just doesn't work now-a-days. The mortgage notes are high. There's arguments all the time between us, with Sally about college. It's just a mess." Hank looked at the machine sculpting his father's heartbeat and in the peaks and valley saw his life as it was years ago . . .

"Now did I say you could buy that?" Daddy's voice boomed from the other room.

"I wanted it," Madear defended in a soft cooing voice.

Hank looked across the wobbly kitchenette table at his older brother James-D. His hair was jet black and naturally laid on his head in curls and waves. It was starting to thin in the front just a little like Daddy's. His nose was delicately shaped as was his chin. His skin was smooth and the same color as the grits mixed with butter now on his spoon. Hank looked at the grits and salt pork on his plate. You're bigger than me and the oldest here, cause Danny in Memphis! You ought to say something! You won't though, cause you're Daddy's favorite!

"TooT! TooT!" Tinker said, playing with his knife and spoon like they were two competing trains.

James-D reached over and grabbed the knife and fork. "Stop making all that noise Black Boy!"

"I work all damn day on two jobs and you don't do nothing all day!" Daddy's voice shouted.

Tinker's face squinted up. "Give me back my trains James-D!" His face was dark brown and shiny and his eyes sparkled. "Give me."

"I stay home with the kids!" Madear whined again softly.

Hank winced.

"Hey Hank," James-D said, "look at little Roy playing with the cards on the floor. Flipping them over for Blackjack just like Daddy and them at the card game last night!"

Their baby brother smiled, bumps that looked like mosquito bites knotted his teething gums. Saliva dribbled down the bib tucked tight under his chin. His tiny hands flipped the cards over. His face was a beautiful toasty brown and loose curls as big as eggs were nestled in the top of his head.

"Hey gambling man!" Stan shouted playfully as he walked into the kitchen. He tapped little Roy on the back of the head. Stan was tall with long, strong legs. His muscular body was shaped like a funnel from the waist up. He stroked his chest, "I'm hungry and I hope y'all saved me some food."

"If you get up late, you get what's left!" James-D said finishing the last of his food.

"Aww, man!" Stan said looking at the two strips of isolated salt pork in the frying pan, then over at the grits barely covering the bottom of the pot. "This is not enough!"

"I work two jobs! TWO JOBS to take care of you and the boys!"

"Y'all sure are dirty. Could've saved me more than this!" Stan said, his big metal spoon making a scraping sound against the bottom of the pot.

"I want my trains back!" Tinker yelled tucking his wrists under his chin. James-D, telling Daddy on you James-D. Tinker licked out his tongue.

Daddy's shouting got louder. "I'm not talking about it anymore now, it goes back!"

"I saw that!" James-D said, raising his open hand.

Tinker winced and closed his eyes.

"I WANT IT!" Madear shouted back.

"Whack—Whack!"

They heard their mother crying.

Tinker opened his eyes. "My poor Madear."

James-D lowered his hand and sat down. He rolled up the sleeves of his white cotton shirt and leaned back in the chair. Tired of this arguing over money!

Stan was now moving to sit beside James-D. When I get a job I'm going to buy Madear all kinds of dresses.

Hank looked around at his brothers. "I'm tired of this! I'm telling Daddy he better stop!"

Stan stared at Hank. "You went to bed normal and woke up crazy."

"Shut-up! I'm the third oldest behind Danny and James-D. I'm almost a man!" Hank turned to go out of the room, then he stopped to get something. He grabbed a steak knife and ran out of the kitchen.

"Aww man!" James-D jumped up from the table, grabbing Stan by the shoulder. "C'mon, we've got to stop him."

Tinker grabbed his knife and fork back. "Ah-ha! Got my trains!"

Stan moved to follow James-D. He grabbed a piece of salt pork with a retreating hand and shoved it in his mouth.

"Where y'all going?" Tinker said scooting the knife and fork along the table.

"To get killed," Stan said rounding the kitchenette table.

"I wanna get killed too!"

"Stay there, Black Boy!" Stan shouted from the other room. He headed down the narrow hallway. Toy trucks and stuffed animals were scattered on the floor. The plastic runner beneath his feet made him slide with each step. Coats hanging from hooks mounted high in the wall made the hallway look dark. There was an old calendar from '42, frayed at the edges and brown, with a picture of Jesus Christ on it balanced against the wall on top of an oak table. Baseball and basketball trophies looked like hills lining the other tables in the hall. Stan turned the corner, stepped into the bedroom and stood behind James-D. He peeped over his shoulder. Hank had the knife behind his back and Madear was on the bed with her head down. What's he doing? Stan asked by pressing his body against his brother's back.

James-D hunched his shoulders.

Out of the corner of his eye, Hank could see his brothers in the doorway watching. Can't chicken out now, they'll never let me forget it. Daddy's just staring at me. God, don't look so mean Daddy. You the one wrong! Hank cleared his throat. "Daddy," he stopped surprised at the weak sound. "Daddy, don't hit Madear no more!"

Madear looked up from the bed. Her big brown eyes were surrounded by red. Her powder-colored face was spotted with red and the anxiety curling her lips downward made her look like a sad clown. Madear's chest fluttered as she tried to stop crying. Her soft reddish-brown hair was falling in her face.

"You're so pretty, Madear!" Hank whispered softly.

"WHAT DID YOU SAY TO ME?" Daddy shouted rising.

"Shit!" Stan whispered dragging the syllable out long and hard.

"What y'all doing in here!" Tinker said skipping into the doorway.

"Get back!" Stan took his foot and slammed the door in his face.

Thump!

"Waaa!" Tinker cried from behind the door.

"Man!" James-D held his breath. He turned his head quickly. "Stan, I'll keep Daddy off of him, you just grab Hank and get him out of here!"

Hank pulled the knife out. "Daddy if you hit Madear again, I'm going to kill you!"

Daddy glared at Hank in disbelief.

Stan turned around and opened the door. Tinker was now sitting on the floor in the hallway with his head down.

"Boy, I'll knock your head off," Daddy said finally coming to grips with his anger. His hands rose and clutched the air.

"Now!" James-D shouted as he tackled his father and they fell back on the bed. Stan grabbed Hank, spun him around and shoved him out the door. "Go-go-go!"

"Right! Right!" Hank said skipping along sideways.

"Get off of me James-D! Hank, come back here goddamn it!" Daddy shouted.

"He didn't mean it!" Madear cried.

"Boy, get back here cause I'm going-get-get off me James-D!" Daddy said pushing him over to the floor.

Hank stopped at the front door.

Stan stared at him: "Will you go? James-D can't hold him but so long!"

"No, I'm just going to face him," Hank said dropping his hand from the doorknob. "He'll respect me if I face him."

"He will KILL YOU if you face him!"

"Well, that'll be more food for you!" Hank said jokingly. He winked at Stan.

"You're stupid–but you sure got heart boy!" Stan said stepping aside.

By now Daddy was in the doorway of the bedroom. Hank stopped three feet in front of him. He opened his mouth but only dry air came out.

Daddy grabbed him by the shirt and swung him around into the closet door of the hallway.

"Daddy!" Stan shouted grabbing his own head with both hands.

"No!" Madear called from the doorway, with James-D behind her.

The doorknob was pressing against the small of Hank's back. He struggled to contain the pain. Don't show it–feel strong. Hank stared at his father. "Do what you gonna do, Daddy."

"Don't you ever tell me nothing about my wife! That's my motherfucking wife! Understand!"

Hank nodded.

James-D moved from behind Madear, tense in anticipation at what would happened next.

Daddy grabbed Hank by the neck and pulled him into the living room.

He pushed him down on the couch and sat next to him. Hank looked straight ahead. The doorway was crowded: Madear, James-D, Stan and Tinker peeping from behind James-D's legs. Daddy reached under the cocktail table and grabbed two shot glasses and a bottle of whiskey. He screwed off the top.

"Goddamn!" James-D whispered running his hands through his hair.

Daddy's gonna give me a drink! He wants me to drink with him! Hank felt his heart start to pound. The insides of his pants pockets stuck to his sweaty thighs.

Stan put his hands on his hips. He's giving Hank a drink like he does his friends--like he's a man! I can't never figure out these crazy niggas in this house!

Daddy poured the liquor and slid the glass to Hank.

Hank picked it up and blushed. Then he glanced over at the folks crowded in the doorway and sat up higher. He nodded to his father and they both drank. The bitter taste scraped the walls of his throat as it went down. Strong! Strong! But Hank relished the taste of it. He dropped the glass back on the table. Daddy did the same. Hank took the bottle and poured another round.

Daddy smiled, "You're more like me than I thought boy."

Now, Hank's hands squeezed the rail even tighter as he pushed back out again. I want to be strong like you Daddy. I want to talk to you again, but you're dying and what can I-can I . . .

"Excuse me," a voice behind him said. The nurse stepped into the room. "The visiting hours are over now."

Hank looked down at him. He bent over and kissed his shoulder again, "See ya later Daddy."

*****

James-D felt the misty rain on the back of his neck. He angrily flipped up the collar of his shirt and undid two more buttons in the front. James-D's arms were getting flabby and his barrel chest had already slipped down around his waist. They promised me and Daddy! I'll check one last bar. James-D felt his throat throbbing as he breathed through his mouth. He looked around. The street was lined with store-front liquor stores, spirit shops, churches and cleaners. Some were boarded up and others seemed to be advertising peeling paint more than anything else. James-D kicked empty beer cans into the crowded gutter, but the sounds couldn't drown out his father's voice from weeks ago . . .

"Promise me James-D! Promise me?" Daddy said in the hospital.

"I promise Daddy," James-D said, shocked at seeing his father cry for the first time.

Daddy's face was swollen, waxy and his paralyzed arms and legs sticking out made him look like a plastic doll. Daddy blinked. Water filled his eyes.

James-D dropped his eyes to the plate of food on top of the hospital stand. He picked up the spoon and began stirring the lumpy mashed potatoes.

"Why? Why they don't come and see me? I was good to all seven of my boys! I raised all of y'all except Danny! And I made sure his Momma had money to take care of him in Memphis!"

Stirring faster.

"I raised y'all and did the best I could--worked two and three jobs so y'all could have. Won't come se-se-see me!" Daddy swallowed. Then his mouth slowly opened like a creaking door, "UGH! Why—because they don't love me!"

The potatoes were now a soupy mess. James-D talked to them while trying to keep them from running into the beets: "Stop it."

"Promise you'll bring them out here to see me? Call Danny in Memphis and tell him again that I'm bad sick! You the one I always depended on. I always depended on you James-D, so I always gave you a little more—remember?"

James-D stopped stirring and let the potatoes run. He could hear Hank's teenaged voice . . . .

"How come James-D gets to stay out longer, gets more money to spend?" Hank asked. He was sitting on the edge of the bottom bunk bed. Hank watched James-D as his father stood in front of the dresser, opening a box from Max's clothing store. Hank pushed: "Huh Daddy?"

"Because he helps take care of you younger boys and he's older," Daddy said turning around looking puzzled at Hank.

"But he's only a year older than me! And he doesn't look after the boys anymore than me!" Hank whined, falling back on the bunk beds.

Daddy unfolded the crisp, new white shirts. "James-D, I know you like these shirts—won a little in cards and got them for you."

James-D grabbed them and hugged his father around the neck, "Thank you, Daddy!"

"How come I can't go to the center?" Hank asked.

"The boys there are big Hank! They're big, strong boys like James-D." Daddy said looking pridefully at James-D.

James-D could see the reflection of Hank's face sagging behind his back. He smiled.

"Now, don't forget that I'm depending on you to help me tomorrow on that side job I have. You'll help me load the truck and figure out the billing."

"Okay, Daddy. I won't stay out too late," James-D said still primping in the mirror.

Hank folded his arms and sucked his teeth, thinks he's something!

"Don't forget James-D now. I'm depending on you," Daddy had said dropping his hand on his shoulder.

James-D looked up and saw Daddy crying. His face was dry and the tears were getting hung up on flakes of peeling skin. Suddenly, there was a moan from his throat that sounded like nails being pulled from a board: "Ugghhh!"

"Goddamn it!" James-D squeezed the spoon and he could feel the metal cutting a welt across the palm of his hand. "Daddy, I promise I'll–we'll all be here next Sunday–spend the whole day with you, hear?"

Daddy nodded in between tears, "Un-huh!"

"Un-huh!" James-D said now looking through the glass window of the bar. He saw Tinker sitting at the bar in the back and Benny crouched in the corner of one of the booths. He stepped into the doorway and slammed his hand against the wooden border of the door. The glass in the center popped and rattled. The woman behind the bar winced then hunched her shoulders, "Don't tear the door down, baby!"

"Shut up Nita!"

She put her hands on her hips and shifted her weight to the back of her heels. Nita's hair was a dyed salt and pepper and combed from the back underneath. Her front teeth stuck out over her bottom lip. The red satin dress she wore hugged her body. Nita wore her best dress on the first weekend of the month to entice bigger tips from the men who had just gotten their checks. Nita hunched her breast up with the bottom of her wrists and headed down toward the open end of the bar. Out of the corner of her eye she saw James-D talking to Tinker. His voice was making a steady, even rise.

"Man, y'all was suppose to go see Daddy today!" James-D said angrily to Tinker.

"Hey James-D!" Benny said falling over out of the booth. The back of his hand dusted the tile floor. His head, bald in the front and gray around the sides, was resting all the way back against the torn, vinyl seat. "Daddy real sick, James-D!"

"He's a little out of it," Tinker said calmly, looking into his glass of beer. His body was a little heavy in spots, but pretty much in good shape. His hair was cut short on the sides and full on the top. Worry lines tracked his brow and the sides of his face. He played with the snap of his watch band while talking. "I know you're mad James-D, but hey be cool!"

"Be cool? Y'all just sitting here drinking, while Daddy lying up there in the hospital!"

"Daddy's in a coma and the doctor says there's no hope," Tinker said calmly. I can't stand to see him down. But Tinker was unable to express this to his brother. "There's no hope, James-D."

"That's because y'all killing him by not going to see him! He doesn't want to live cause of y'all," James-D shouted at the top of his lungs.

"Naw, how we killing him? You always been his favorite and now I guess you God to judge?" Tinker's jaws were fluttering as his throat blew air up into this mouth. He pressed his lips together tightly.

"I'm telling it like it is! You and Benny and all y'all should be there for him and you aren't! Y'all promised to go out to see him today!"

"I don't want to see him, okay? Okay! And if it ain't okay with you so fucking what!" Tinker yelled sliding away from bar.

"Poor Daddy! Poor Daddy!" Benny said his arm still swinging on the floor.

James-D moved toward Tinker: "Y'all are going to see him, if I got to kick everybody's ass!"

"Hey Hal get out here quick!" Nita yelled toward the back. she was now on top of the bar, bent over shouting: "Hurry !"

"Go on, hear James-D?" Tinker said glaring.

"You make me go on, goddamn it!" James-D said stepping closer.

"Come on with it then!"

"That's it boys," a gray haired man named Hal said as he stepped between them. His face was black and shiny like ink. He wore a knit shirt that zipped from the mid-chest up. The top of his ears were burnt from cold winds and heat. His hands were big and hard and scaly. "I knowed your Daddy a long time and I know he wouldn't like this."

"That you Hal?" Benny said looking at him upside down. "Yeah, that's you!"

James-D went to push Hal out of the way.

"Me and your Daddy are about the same age, boy!" Hal smiled and the too big dentures made him look like a horse baying."Go on home son."

"Forget it! Forget it! I'm getting out of here," James-D said knocking over chairs as he headed back out the front door.

Hal shook his head and turned to Tinker, "Sit down and finish your drink. Then you can leave and take Benny too cause he done had enough."

Tinker just looked at Hal, his mind jumbled with thoughts of escape as Hal walked away.

"Hey, Tinker, where'd everybody go?" Benny asked still hanging upside down.

"Shut-up!"

"Hey-Hey," Benny said almost stuttering. "He-ey, I'll kick your upside down ass boy!"

Tinker laughed to himself and took a sip of beer. It was flat now. He looked down at his brother: "You haven't beat me in years, not since that last time . . . ."

"Boy who got a hold of you?" Daddy asked stopping his work. His arm was back, the saw's teeth halfway through the wood. Sweat was pouring down his face, neck, and arms.

"Benny, Daddy!" Tinker's lip was throbbing and his cheeks stung. Under his left eye a dark ring was appearing.

Daddy walked over and started checking Tinker's face. His hands were sweaty and rough. They felt like brillo pads washing over his face.

"Ouch, Daddy!"

"You'll live. But it looks like you didn't even fight back."

"I was trying to block him, but Benny is just too fast Daddy!"

"Un-huh, how come you didn't FIGHT him back?" Daddy asked sitting down on the wood pile next to his work bench.

Tinker wiped at his lip, relieved that it wasn't swelling. He stuck his hands in his pocket and kicked the gravel in the yard behind their building. He looked up at the outdoor back porches hanging crooked from the scant apartments.

"I asked you a question? I mean, Benny's older than you, but he isn't bigger than you anymore."

Tinker frowned and worked his jaws before breathing, "I know I'm just as strong as he is but . . . well . . . he's something more than me!"

Daddy walked over and put his arm around his shoulder. "He is NOTHING more than you. None of you boys is better than the other. I might give one of you more or praise one of you more sometimes but that's because that son is working harder, trying harder, trying to do something. But none of my boys is better than the other. But if you think that—you'll start believing it and your brothers will start to believe it too. You're as good as everybody else."

"But he's always calling me `Black Boy' because I'm darker than everybody else—got all the kids doing it, even little Roy's doing it now! I don't like it Daddy."

"Tell you what, we'll fix that up right now! Where is Benny now?"

"Everybody's at the Catholic school in the center," Tinker said listening closely. Benny's gonna catch it now! "Want me to run and tell him you said come here?"

"Nope," Daddy said squeezing his shoulder tighter. "Where is Florida on the map?"

"Huh?"

"Show me Florida on the map with your hand!"

"It's down here," Tinker said using his right hand.

"Good! I want you to go over there and as soon as Benny says black boy I want you to reach down and get your fist outta Florida and hit him dead in the mouth as hard as you can."

Tinker tried to pull away. "But he'll beat me up again!"

Daddy held him close. "No he won't because you'll have the first lick in and after that you'll be fighting back. He'll respect you and everybody in there will. They'll know what you don't like and they'll know they'll have a fight on their hands if they mess with you. Besides that, you're getting whupped anyway, right?"

"Yeah."

"But this way, you'll get some licks in. And I know for a FACT that your bruises will be gone tomorrow. As light as Benny is, he'll be looking like hell for the rest of the week. He'll wish he was a black boy then! Ha-Ha!"

"Okay, Daddy!" Tinker said smiling. "He sho' do stay red as a beet for days." He turned and started heading out the yard.

"Hey Tinker," Daddy called lining up his saw again. "Do Benny still drop his left before he punch with it all the time?"

Tinker stopped. "Huh?"

"I say, do Benny still drop his left before he punch with it?"

"Oh, yeah Daddy. He still do," Tinker said. He turned and started jogging away.

The inside of the gym was packed with teenagers and a few folks in their early twenties. There were wooden bleachers on the north side of the room and the hard, glazed floor seemed to vibrate and pop with each bounce of the basketball. There were a dozen or so boys on the floor playing a half-court game. A group of small girls were playing hop–scotch on a plywood board laid out by one of the priest behind the bleachers. On the other side of the room the oldest of the crowd were sitting around talking. Some girls were leaning between their boyfriends legs, heads resting underneath their chins. Some were bopping and others, loud and off key, were trying to imitate their favorite group. Tinker saw Benny and Stan sitting in the corner with their friends. Tinker started walking over.

His knees locked and a cool, beaded perspiration stitched his brow. Then Daddy's words began ringing in his ears: Florida! Florida! Tinker found strength and walked over and stood right in front of Benny.

Benny jumped off the bleacher, the bottom of his shoes smacked against the floor: "Man, I thought I told you Black Boy–"

Florida! Whack! Tinker's hand felt like it was going to fall off. He looked down at Benny now sprawled out at his feet.

"Ha! Look at that boy! I knew you had it in you," Stan said jumping up and down laughing. "Y'all get back now. Give 'em room."

Benny grabbed his chin, shook it off, then got up. He pulled his hands up into tight fists and began circling. "I'm going to kick your butt like I always do!" And he circled.

"Watch him!"

Tinker circled in the opposite direction.

"Fight! Fight!"

The gym was vibrating with shouts now.

Benny took two quick steps in, and dropped his left.

Step right: Swing! Tinker looked down and Benny was sprawled out at his feet again. His lip was bleeding now. Tinker looked around at the crowd. They were perfectly still, lifeless with mouths open. Tinker looked down at Benny and breathed for the crowd's benefit: "C'mon and go some more chump!"

That brought the crowd back to life. "Oh!" they moaned.

Benny got up and rushed him."Aww! I'm going kick your . . . ."

Tinker back peddled and threw two punches that glazed Benny's chin. Dropping that left. Step and swing! Benny hit the back of the wooden bleachers. His shirt was spotted with blood. Benny put his hand up to signal enough. Tinker dropped his fists. He could barely feel them. He spoke loudly over the noise: "My name is Albert, but Tinker suits me just fine."

Now, Tinker slid the glass away from him toward the edge of the bar.

"Hey Tinker," a voice from behind him called. "Benny's over there snoring!"

"Huh?"The man looked familiar but Tinker couldn't really place him.

"You'd better take him home."

"I'll take him home in a minute," Tinker said turning back around.

"Hey brother, he looks . . . ."

Tinker turned around, slid off the stool, and got in the man's face. "You ain't my brother. I got enough brothers–too many brothers. I got five here that are getting on my last nerves and I got one in Memphis I don't even know, so don't brother me OKAY!"

"I'm sorry," the man said backing away. "Damn I didn't think you'd get like that. We all used to hang up in the center and I thought I'd say something is all. My fault!"

Guilt and remorse swept over Tinker. "Naw, it's my fault. Sorry. I'm taking him home now." Tinker walked over and grabbed Benny under the arms and pulled. His feet slid and hit the floor like a load of bricks.

"SNZX! Huh? Huh?" Benny moaned sleepily.

"C'mon, you need to sleep it off at home. Tinker said swinging his head under his arm. "You need a shower too!"

"Where we going? Huh?"

"You're going to bed," Tinker said stopping outside in the doorway to get a better grip on Benny's waist. Tinker hunched Benny's body up with his shoulders, slipped his fingers into the belt loops, and began carrying him down the street.

"I want to see Daddy!" Benny mumbled. "Cause I haven't been to see him. I haven't been to see him because I'm . . . ." Not even the liquor could free his voice to admit his fear. "I'm drunk!"

"I know, now shut up!" Tinker said turning the corner.

"Get me to bed Tinker, cause that's how Daddy got ruined. He came home drinking too much and slipped and fell down the steps. Just ruined him! Paralyzed him from the neck down!" Benny clutched the back of Tinker's neck. "I carried Daddy downstairs because the ambulance was taking too long. I walked all the way to the hospital with him!"

"I know, Madear told us."

"Don't let me fall, now!" Benny said softly. And his mind drifted back to years ago. . . .

"What's the matter with you boy, you scared?" Daddy asked Benny?

"Naw, Daddy I'm not scared," Benny answered looking up at the board stretched across the two ladders spaced twenty-feet apart. There was a big, metal bucket full of water up there and two torn plaid shirts to be used as rags. Man, I could fall and break my neck climbing up there. Benny stuck his hands, palms out, into his back pockets.

"You can't wash the windows by just looking at them Benny," Daddy said. He was sitting on the folded down door of the old station wagon.

"Daddy, you've been doing this as a side job all these years?"

"Yep! And you know why?" he said unloading a box of soap and pulling out more rags. "BECAUSE I don't have a high school education, that's why!"

Benny looked over, pursed his lips in a sneer and thought, You think you slick Daddy.

"Well, go on. You said you didn't want to finish high school and that you wanted to work—well work. And remember, take it slow going up."

Benny walked over to the ladder and started to climb. He stared at his father's bent back. "Heading up Daddy."

"Okey-dokey!" Daddy said not turning around.

Benny continued to climb the ladder. Hand over hand. He felt the legs move, "Daddy, the ladder's shaking!"

"That's your imagination!" he said not turning around. "I'm just fixing up this bucket over here—you go ahead!"

"Shoot Daddy! This crazy old ladder and we ain't hardly making no money on this job! You hear me?!"

"You don't get paid much without a high school education! Okey-dokey, go on up!"

Benny started climbing up the ladder quickly. I'll show you! The legs started to slide and he kept going. Suddenly, he felt his foot slip. "Daddy!" he yelled tumbling back down. The ground was hot and hard as it baked his back. Pain numbed his body.

"You all right?" Daddy said looking down at him. "Benny! Benny!"

"Yeah, I'm okay Daddy," Benny said dazed. He strained his eyes and tried to shift through the waxy blur in front of him. Benny felt his father checking his arms and legs with his hands. He could hear his father's wrists creaking. Daddy you getting old, man.

"Boy, I thought you'd get tired. I never thought you'd fall! Nothing broken?"

"Naw, Daddy nothing's broken. And I still don't want to go to school."

Daddy patted his chest: "Alright boy." His face looked kind of sad and tired. "I'm not going to make you go back to school if you want that badly to be out. I know you making a mistake and I'm just going to have to let you make it. . . ."

"Sho' was a mistake Daddy !" Benny mumbled now.

"What?" Tinker said pulling off his brother's shoes. One brother tries to beat me up and I've got to tuck the other one in bed.

"Hey, Daddy's dying man! What we GONNA DO MAN!"

"Sssh!" Tinker said. "You'll wake up Madear!"

"SSsh! You'll wake up Madear," Benny repeated letting himself fall back on the bed. "Daddy!" he whispered.

Tinker folded his feet up and over into the bed. He pulled the old, orange spread tight and then rolled Benny over twice.

"Daddy! Daddy," Benny hummed in the darkness as he rocked himself to sleep under the covers.

*****

"RRRrnng!"

Roy pulled the pillow over his head and defended his ears against the piercing sound. He didn't want to talk to anyone after losing big in the card game the night before.

"RRRng!"

"Madear! Benny answer the telephone!" he moved the pillow to shout, then tucked it back.

"RRRng!"

"Shit!" Roy tossed the pillow on the floor and stood up. He started walking past the dresser to answer the phone that was on top of the television. He stopped and glanced at his reflection.

"RRRng!"

Roy ran his hand across his bald head. I'm not going to walk around looking old—just shave it all off!

"RRRng!"

Roy yanked up the receiver and yelled, "Yeah!"

It was as if a hand was pulling at his face. Roy closed his eyes as pain alternately simmered the top of his head and the bottom of his feet. He slapped his forehead and popped his body up on the tips of his toes: "Daddy!" He hung up the receiver and grabbed his mouth to stop his teeth from chattering.

Roy looked around—clothes, put on clothes and go tell everybody. Aww, Daddy! Tears were starting to fill his eyes. Shoes . . . . where are my shoes . .

MOTHERFUCKIN' SHOES . . . . He spotted a pair in the corner. "There they are, be cool man!" he said forcing a smile. All-all, ex-excited! "Daddy!" he moaned loudly. "SSsh!" he hushed himself in the empty room. Roy grabbed a shirt and pulled it over his head. My Daddy's dead! I didn't go see him! Lord, Daddy! He grabbed a pair of jeans laying across a raggedy rocking chair. The belt buckles clanked as he slipped them on. "I just couldn't stand to see you hurting Daddy!" Roy grabbed his basil cap off the corner dresser and slipped it on his shaved head. Lord, make him understand. Roy ran to the door and skipped down the steps.

Outside the morning sun was sending down punishingly hot waves. It was already 85 degrees and it wasn't even noon. Daddy's dead! God, glad Madear wasn't home to get that call! Lord, Daddy! Jesus! Shut–up, boy you don't never go to church and Daddy never went! Daddy! I'm never going to see you again. The thought set off an avalanche of tears. Roy leaned against the side of the brick two-flat. Wobbly, hoarse words from years ago came to him. . . .

"Hey Roy, your old man is looking for you!" a voice behind him called.

A teenaged Roy ignored the words of the rival shooter, sure he was trying to break his concentration. Roy stared at the crumpled pile of dollar bills bunched up in the corner of the gym floor. A group of girls were acting as shields so the priest across the gym couldn't see that they were gambling.

"Need seven!" Roy shouted, wishing and blowing on the dice as if they were stubborn birthday candles.

"Boy, is you gonna take all day or what!" Mel said nudging him with his left elbow. Mel had his right palm pressed against his face. He always did. He had been badly scarred as a child when he tipped over a skillet of grease looking for a piece of his mother's fried chicken. "C'mon Roy!"

"C'mon bones!" Roy knew he was sweating but he didn't want to lose the feeling. The dice in his hand seemed to be moving on their own. Roy picked the spot on the wall where he wanted them to hit. His shoes were spit shined and he could see the white of the dice reflected in the toes. The corners of the dice were now biting his palms. The crease in his pants sliced the floor as he leaned over and started shaking the dice. Sounds just like I got a snake in my hand. "C'mon baby strike! Ha!" Roy's hand released them and they spun out and sat up.

"Seven!" Mel shouted. "That goddamn Roy has won all the money!"

"Ha! Yeah!" Roy shouted jumping up and down in a squat position like a frog. "I'm too much!" He reached over to grabbed the money.

"Boy, you gonna make me hurt you!" Daddy said grabbing him by the back of the collar and pulling.

Roy felt his legs unfolding and the dry air slapping against his empty palms.

"I done told you and told you not to stay out all times of night gambling. I done told you to stop cutting school to gamble!" Daddy slung him against the bleachers.

Roy winced, then began pleading with his eyes. He looked around at the others starting to watch. Don't hit me in front of my friends, Daddy. Don't embarrass me anymore! His heart pounding made it hard to swallow.

Daddy's eyes soften. "C'mon let's go home," he said turning walking away.

Roy followed behind him at a distance. Daddy's back was tense and sagging around the shoulders. His legs seemed to drag just a little before they took the next step. Daddy headed out the door. The metal clanked against the brick side of the building. Roy winced feeling the intensity of his father's anger in the distance stretched between them. But Roy was angry too. He was sixteen, almost seventeen. He could win more in the gym in a day than he could in a week working with his father after school.

Daddy crossed the street and turned the corner.

Yep, I'm just gonna tell him that I need to hang out with the fellahs and make some easy cash. Roy turned the corner. "Hey, Dad—"

"Don't you ever!" Daddy yelled swinging his hand.

Duck—left. Roy dodged the blow.

"You stop all this mess!" Daddy shouted again trying to corner him.

Roy bounced around. He was amazed at how hard his father was breathing.

"You get good grades in school and you could go to college!" Daddy shouted trying to grab him. He missed and crashed his shoulder into the wall.

"Dawg Daddy!"

"What you grinning at?" Daddy asked breathing heavily, leaning against the wall.

"You Daddy!" Roy said grinning some more. "It's over, man."

"Go on home boy," Daddy said still trying to catch his breath.

Roy grinned wider, "Sure thing, Daddy."

Tears blinded him now as he struggled to push himself away from the brick building he was leaning against. The mortar scraped the outline of his ear. Daddy! His feet were dragging making a swishing sound against the pavement. Roy saw the body in front of him. He was crying so hard now that it sounded like he was laughing. He stopped in the middle of the street. The smell of cooking pork made its way to his senses through his open mouth. Find the words.

"Honk! Honk!"

Roy didn't move.

The car swerved around him.

Find the words. Roy tasted the tears as the body moved closer to him. Find the words. Roy cried, "James-D, Daddy's dead! Daddy's dead!"

*****

"Hey Tinker, you get that end!" Stan shouted.

"Right," Tinker said slipping the white gloves on.

"Me and Benny are over here and Roy got that back end," Stan directed. "Damn it's hot out here today—must be a thousand degrees! Danny, get in front with James-D since y'all the oldest."

Danny looked at the casket, resting in the opened door of the hearse.

"Danny!" Stan shouted again.

Danny looked up. "Yeah, Stan ?"

"Grab the front handle, you're the oldest," Stan repeated moving to his position.

"Okay." The oldest! Brother, I don't even know when your birthday is! Danny slipped on the white gloves he had been given. He looked across at James-D who was already staring straight ahead, hands clutching the handle of the casket. And what's your favorite color? Huh? Danny shook his head. He looked across and back at Benny. Man, do you know that I'm crazy about candy corn and peanuts? Huh? Naw, you don't. Sweat was dripping down Danny's face now. He looked behind him at Hank. The old man really put his mark on you!

"Ready!"

Danny stepped up and grabbed the handle.

"Lift!"

The seven brothers walked as one.

Step . . . Stop.

I'm leading the processional for a father I never knew.

Step . . . Stop.

Danny looked down at the gray casket. The sun gleaming against the steel reflected up, burning his eyes. He turned away. Daddy why didn't you come to Memphis and get me so I could be with y'all? I got six brothers and don't know. . . . Don't know nothing. I don't know YOU Daddy. What did you like to do, huh?

Step . . . Stop.

Did you like to wrestle with them on the floor? Was you strict? Momma got money to help support me but a check can't take a kid to a baseball game, Daddy! Did you ever think of that?

Step . . . Stop.

This is crazy! James-D called and said you were bad sick and to come visit. I was sorry but I wasn't hurt because it was like I knew the name, Daddy, but I-I didn't have nothing to go with it really. But now, today, here with my brothers I feel I could've loved you cause they're crying and all these folks keep saying how special you were. The mailman patted me on the back and said you were a great man—now can you beat that? THE

MAILMAN knew you better than me! Why-why-why? God, it must . . . MUST mean . . . um, all this GOT TO mean that you were worth loving. And last night, Benny and Stan and them were telling stories about you and I had nothing to say, nothing to tell. And I know they were giving the stories to me but I just wish I wasn't getting your love from my brothers like a hand-me-down shirt. Daddy . . . Daddy, I don't even know you and God know's I wish that I had and . . . and, Jesus, if you looking down Daddy . . . I don't know, just look down Daddy and know that I'm gonna miss the chance to know you now more than ever.

Stop.

They eased the casket atop the metal bed protruding from the empty grave. It squeaked and dropped a few inches. The people around the grave were bunched together like weeping willows. The sun was beating down, the grass was brown, and there was no air—just tears and groans. Fingers clutching a black book, sprinkled dust and hummed: "Naked we come into this world and naked we go out . . . Ashes to ashes . . . . dust to dust!"

Click!

The casket started to lower. The sons stood in a line around the edge of the grave. One by one they took the roses from their lapels and dropped them into the grave: Bye, Daddy.▲

John R. Keene Jr. was born in St. Louis, MO and attended Harvard. He won a Massachusetts Artists Foundation Fellowship for 1990-1991. His work has appeared in *Callaloo* and *Shooting Star*, and in the anthology *Brother To Brother* (Alyson, 1991) and will appear in *Muleteeth* and *Other Countries*. He is a member-in-earnest of the Dark Room Writers Collective of Boston.

"Conscience, consanguinity, consensus, concord." ▲

NOBLE MCDANIEL'S DAMBALAH

by JOHN R. KEENE JR.

POPPOW! Off go the blasts like a mad symphony of firecrackers: POW! POPPOW! POWPOWPOW! The armoire glass cracks, the front window and the mirror shatter, the shade and draperies flutter from their perch, plaster splatters from the walls, the portrait of her late husband Osyrus leaps into the air and, with the precision of a diver, angles straight to the floor. POWPOW! Within seconds of the first blast Noble hurls herself, unrobed and wigless, prone to the threadbare carpet. POW! A bullet ricochets off the cast-steel hinge of the closet door, scattering over her prostrate form the hundred porcelain shards that were her bedside lamp. POW! A stray bullet shivers the polished surface of her dressing table, dispersing perfumes and powders in all directions. Flush to the floor she lies, her eyelids riveted, fists balled, jaws clenched, as the fusillade plays on, POWWOP!

Silence as she lies, her head one with the hand-knitted rug, her knotted form rigid as the floor beneath. Am I alive? Am I breathing? Her chest neither rises nor falls, her diaphragm tight as a lead washer, unmoving, her insides empty of all breath. Am I dead? Am I dead? Her insides empty, her body still as bone: I'm dead. No way all of them bullets missed me. I've died and am passing over, so like all the faithful come to the end of the road, I'm pledging this soul to Jesus and waiting for the signs: the blinding Light; the choir of His angels; the burning Bush; the Ancestors draped in the finest silks and jewels, returning to welcome me on over there. But as she lays there, the debris mapping the space around her, nothing happens: there is no blinding Light, there is no choir of Angels, there are no Ancestors calling out to her, no burning Bush or descent of doves or God's voice, in whatever form, nothing. She waits a little longer. Nothing.

Then, I'm alive, Noble realizes, yanking a quick breath from the powdery murk above her what happened? Was I hit? Shot? Her body plank-stiff, paralyzed? Either from wounds or from fear she is not sure, but with each gasp of air, she repeats to herself, I must be alive, I must be alive, I must be alive. Before she can reason the extent of this "alive," something deep within her rises, swells up, bursts out to the loud slience: "Thank you Lord Jesus, lay me near thy cross I'm alive." As each word leaps from her lips, the wind rushes in, whistling its assent. I may be wounded, but I'm not dead. I'm not dead. They did not kill me. Praise Jesus-Son-of-God. Bullets flying every which way, but I'm not dead. I'm not dead. Praise Heavenly Father God of Mercy, I'm not dead.

Was I hit? You can't tell right off, her sister Precious had once told her, because of the shock. But then the pain floods you, just floods you. You been waiting and then you start drowning in it. That's when you know you been shot and if it don't come right away either you dead or you gone have to live. So she waits. And waits and waits, but pain refuses to appear. In fact, for the first time in almost seven years, the length and breadth of her

77-year-old body bring her no pain: I must be paralyzed. Then suddenly her left hand, which had, during the initial hail, melded into her side, stirs from its stoneness. Without heed or contemplation, she brings it to her heart–which is hammering against the wall of her chest–then sweeps it up to her head, to her neck, then around to her back, to her buttocks, to her stomach, to her pelvis. Not one wound. Her eyes focus on that divining hand: no blood. The bullets missed me. Praise Jesus, thank you Lord Almighty, I'm all right.

Pulling herself up from the carpet, she surveys the entire span of her bedroom. A warped arc of some thirteen bullet holes, each the center of a web of cracks, tracks high across the wall facing the front window and her bed. Two other bullet holes, framed by the naked copper casing and the absence of the mirror-glass, gouge the wall to the left of her bed, while two others have splintered the wall to the right. Wind hollers through the bald sash where the bullets came in. On the floor, amid the sea of porcelain, plaster, wood, and lace, floats the shattered portrait of Osyrus. Rolling her head backwards in awe and disgust, she begins to sigh deeply, so deeply that the sigh becomes a grunt then a shriek then explodes as a howl. Before she realizes what is happening, she is howling at the top of her voice, she is snatching the cover off the bed. She is stamping around her room, scattering porcelain and powders about her. Those bastards shoot into my house, *my house*, do *I* know them? No! Nearly killing *me—me*, Noble Antonia Rogers McDaniel—when the target, the one they aiming to get, I know it, the one maybe just one of those bullets just should have hit, that grandson of mine, why *do* I claim him?—Dambalah—whom I took into my house because nobody else in the family would. He drove my babyboy Junie out of this self same house and my Osyrus to an early grave. Whom I, Noble, have done nearly everything for that a grandmother could do; that a mother could do, that a friend or even a saint *would* do. That grandson of mine, that Dambalah, sometimes I swear the very image of the Devil himself—ain't even set foot or soul in this house since nine yesterday morning!

Shaken by her outburst, Noble drops to her bed, growing aware now that only a sheer cotton nightgown covers her nakedness; that her nightscarf has buried itself under the glass and plaster; that neither windowglass nor shade nor draperies separate her now from the early morning gales; and that if her neighbors, or any stranger on the street in fact, stand in the right place outside, they will see her barely clad; nearly bald form clearly lit by the moon and lamp light. As she rolls, shivering, across the bed to the closet to grab her housecoat, she can hear a concert of voices outside. Look at me trying to put on a wig without a mirror in sight. The TV cameras and police gone be here before I know it. I need . . . she reaches into the drawer of her bedtable. Her quivering hand glides over little packages of Extra Strength Tylenol, Advil; over half-empty bottles of Valiums, Lopressins, Imipramine; over a handcarved rosary, which her daughter Eva stole from an Indian church in Mexico; over a cold, brass letter-opener; over a Medicaid statement; and over a crumpled, yellow pack of cigarettes which she had tossed in the back of this drawer six years ago when she finally quit smoking. The TV cameras start whirring, the voices outside grow louder, joined first by a single siren, then a chorus of sirens. Wrapping the housecoat around herself, Noble slides her feet into her slippers, and runs her hand through the contents of the drawer once more. Soon the voices and the sirens are filling the room. After a moment's deliberation, she pulls out the cigarettes and the Imipramine, then starts down the stairs.

*****

Wringing her hands into towel knots, Noble lights up the last cigarette from the pack. In the surface of the kitchen table, which she has three times polished clean, her reflection, haggard and drawn, stares back at her, turning her away in disbelief. They shot into my house! Into MY house, the no-account bastards! And to think, I might never have known these kind of people, shooting into houses and such! Into my house! Seventy-seven years, seventy-seven good years, as a mother, a wife, a grandmother, a great-grandmother, as a teacher, a counselor, a church-going woman. Working hard every day and living a clean life–a Christian life–yet trying to keep up with all the changes in the world. Not staying left back in the Depression or the War like Osyrus or Vietnam like Miss Settle's brother. Moving foward and keeping up. Keeping *on* Junie used to say. Then I look up, and here I am burying myself into the carpet for dear life, while bullets scattering through the air above my head, and the police got the nerve to ask ME if I am dealing drugs or in a gang or feuding with somebody or something else crazy like that. Who would have thought it possible, Lord Today! To think that I worked every day that I could for nearly sixty years trying to make a place for my children and their children. To make sure that they had even when I did not, to ensure that they would never have to experience the terrible things that most folks go through, to guarantee that they was law-abiding, God-fearing, decent people. And now somebody's gone shoot into my house trying to kill that boy–that Dambalah–who's tripping out somewhere in the street. They near about kill me! Where Lord, tell me where, did I go wrong?

Hoping to turn her mind away from all such questions, and from the frigid morning altogether, she tries to concentrate on the blue/gray cigarette smoke rising across the room toward the pantry. Yet her memory will not comply. Summoning the recollection that when her daughter Eva ran off to Mexico, leaving the child all by himself at the Warren Homes with neither a dime nor a scrap of food and no one, knowing what kind of woman his mother was; how she could barely take care of herself. She was such a free spirit and she had not wanted him anyway. She had not wanted any part of any family, not a husband a child, a father, not even her own mother. When no one would take him in after what he had gone through, except me; and when, later on, after the endless fights and arrests, the trouble with every child in the neighborhood and the school, when I could hardly get him to listen to me without Osyrus's help, then all the problems struck *him* dead. Then that earnest, red-haired fifth grade teacher, I forget her name, first asked me if I was familiar with the marijuana and the Angel Dust. How they turn these kids upside-down. She could spot these changes right away and told me she spotted it immediately in his eyes. I claimed that it was all news to me, that I had never seen or heard of such things. When I was a teacher myself and watched it happen to other peoples' children time and time again. . . .

When each time something came up, she did what she thought was right. Trying to go along with it all for so long, even though charity starts at home. He was my real baby. His mother ran away to Mexico with a woman and his daddy was not fit to raise a dog. So what was anybody supposed to expect from the boy. I saw right away he was a slow-learner. Then the integration. Things just fall apart nowadays. I only did what I thought was right. Eva failed so I *had* to make it up to him. Then the drugs and the alcohol. His mama just up and left him. My Lord, the poor child's name alone. How could things help but go wrong. So I chose the only way I knew. In spite of the pleas of teachers, neighbors, friends of my own family that I was creating a monster, but where were they when I needed them. Why wouldn't they so much as lift a finger to help, no sir! So can't a one say that I did not try. Now, Lord, be my witness, one thing is for certain, after this shooting I'm gone have to try my way again. This time Dambalah has got to get out, out he has to go, my own flesh and blood. I can't worry what will they say about me out in the street: that she did not care, that she was a failure twice, Lord you will have to forgive me but. . . Noble drags on the cigarette butt so hard she loses her breath. She erupts in coughs, knocking to the kitchen floor the cup of coffee and the ashtray. . . *he has got to go.*

First thing, Noble remembers, she must call the clinic where she works a few afternoons a week as a youth counselor. Probably they have not heard about the shooting, because the TV does not broadcast this kind of thing immediately, unless somebody dies. Then there is the disaster that was, until 4:26 this morning, her bedroom. Earlier, right after the policemen left, Mary Ann Settle from next door came by and insisted that Noble allow her and her stepfather to come and help clean up. Noble had proudly said no thank you, whereupon Miss Settle insisted, several times, "We're going to help you clean up, that's it". The last "that's it" so firm how could she resist? Now hovering over the mess at her feet, Noble realizes that they will be here soon enough—with the police returning as well. After the ambulances had left and the crowd had thinned, she gave them a statement. But they decided that they would still send two detectives over anyways—procedure—and they wanted to know if he had returned, even though she repeated at least five times, I have not seen him since yesterday. As she bends over to pick up the cup and ashtray, a pang shoots below her breastplate: She must not forget to reschedule her doctor's appointment because her gallstones have been acting up again and two days ago she was sure that she had passed blood, and . . . and above all, she knows, but does not want to admit it, she knows what she has got to do: *he has got to go.*

He will come in through the basement as he always does, after two or three days' absence—normally three is the longest he is gone—around two or so in the afternoon, unable to speak his own name. He will come in through the basement and go straight to his bedroom. Maybe this morning he will have a girl or that friend with him. Maybe he will have his arm in a sling or his leg in a bandage. Maybe there will be a trail of blood leading to the foot of his bedroom door. Maybe . . . but I know that when I am ready, that bedroom directly beneath the pantry is where I'm gone have to go. I can't care what people will say. I know, I know those church folks gone say I'm wrong; I'm the problem and ought to be put away. Junie gone say, like always, that I was wrong from the beginning; that I should have gotten the boy help instead of abetting him; should have put him in a home instead of trying to do the job myself. Miss Settle gone say how could you throw your own kin out into the street. Ms. Noble, no matter what he's done he's still your grandson? But Lord knows, things change, this ain't hardly the world of when I was coming up. You can't just hide things like this anymore. Folks shooting into windows. Even if I was to blame, you can't just hide it, kin or no kin. I refuse to end up like that Inez Goolsby, lying in a pool of blood, shot dead while she knitting a sweater for her great-great-grandson, this I got to do. Abruptly, Noble looks down, spots herself in the puddle of coffee. This I got to do. With the tips of her slippers, she wipes away her reflection, then gathers her housecoat around her waist and heads upstairs, gripping the bannister more tightly with each step. This I got to do.

*****

Although the gold hands of the Belgian watch that Osyrus brought her back from the war tell her that it is 1:30 P.M., her eyes register only the dull blur of casing and background. Focusing, she examines in one wide sweep her living room: the cream lace curtains, the chintz-patterned sofa, the faux-marble coffeetable, the polished dark wood of this old room silent and oblivious, as she once was, to the morning and its violence. Sighing, she recalls what a trial it was to get Miss Settle and her stepfather to leave. She almost did not get a chance to dress. Then, almost as soon as she has thrown on some clothes, the police arrive and they want her to answer all sorts of questions: When was the last time you saw Dambalah? Can you remember any of the names of his associates—X? Y? Z? Have you ever heard the names before? No. Do you know how extensively Dambalah was dealing? No. Tell us anything you know about his doings? Nothing. His habits? Nothing. What about the neighbors, anything, have you seen, have you heard, and on and on.   Before she can answer, they suddenly decide they are satisfied and give her a number to call if she sees or learns of Dambalah's whereabouts.   Yes I'll call you, yes I understand—just to get them all out the door, yes, yes, yes.   Noble walks over to the upright piano whose hood she has adorned with photographs of every member of her family.   Her eyes run from the baby pictures of her sons, Gordon and Junie; to her daughters, Jewel, Naomi, Dolores, Sylvia, Louise, Eva.   Her eyes fix momentarily on this last one: Eva, the mirror-image of Noble herself. From Eva her eyes scurry to the other pictures: her grandchildren by her son Gordon, by her daughters Jewel, Dolores, and Sylvia, her great-granddaughter Ciana, her sister Precious, her brothers Arthur, Varner, and Willie, her mother Valdosta and her father Perry, Osyrus, nieces, nephews, Gordon in the Army, Junie graduating from Morgan State, Louise and her boyfriend in Detroit.   Her eyes take in every photograph quickly, finally stopping upon the only photograph of Dambalah.   About nine years old, he is standing alone behind one of the buildings at the Warren Homes where he and Eva lived right after she had left her first husband, Walter.   Noble looks at Dambalah's tight, soiled outfit, the burning, flame-black eyes that he inherited from his father.   The sunken cheeks and wild hair that he got from Eva.   The little hands clenched tightly into fists.   The skinny body pitched forward in unearthly rage.   Noble looks at the little form glaring back at her from within the black plastic frame, realizing now that even then, as Eva stood on the other side of the lens, Dambalah had already crossed over.   Dambalah, Dambalah why did she have to name the boy after a Voodoo god.   Lord have mercy on him.   She started off wrong and left it all up to me . . . Noble turns away sharply, bringing her hand to her bosom. No matter what I feel, he has got to . . . she turns back to Dambalah, this one thought entering her head: Osyrus's shotgun.   Where did he keep that shotgun?   Where?   Where?   Where?   Not in the front closets, nowhere where anybody would look, because Dambalah never found it, where?

Where?   Noble treads a circle around the living room and as she moves away from the piano, a pain grinds like broken glass in her abdomen.   The fists clenched tightly, the little body ready to spring out of the picture frame.   Where?   Not in the garage, not in the attic, where?   She tries to remember the day Osyrus put it away, "I'm gon put it here so that if ever somethin come up, you will always be eble to get it fore the robbers or the police. . . ."   The watch: 2 P.M.   Where did he put that shotgun?   "I'm gon put it . . ."The little form glares back at her from the other side of the room. "I'm gon put it here . . ."Where? "I'm gon put it here". Here, she remembers, in the bathroom adjoining her bedroom . . . That face, those fists, those eyes that she realizes are Eva's, are her own, dazzling in their fury. Under the floorboards is where that .12-gauge is sleeping, under the floorboards". "He has got to go", Noble screams, slamming the picture down against the piano's black wood. "Either him or me". Clutching her stomach, she heads upstairs to lie down, to pray, to find that shotgun; which she has never handled before and hopes against every hope she will not have to learn how to use now. In her heart she is sure he will never force her to use . . . Under the floorboards. He has got to go.

*****

The fingertips of her right hand, trembling, slide in paces along the well, while her left hand cradles the shotgun. Her heart is tapping out her advance. Eyes closed, Noble moves steadily down the half-lit hallway toward Dambalah's room. When her hand reaches the molding outlining the door to his room, she stops. Her eyes open. They return instinctively to the white watchface, to the position of the gold hands: 7:25 P.M. Though she has not heard him come in, he is surely on the other side of the door. Her heart renews its drumming, her eyes close. As her hand gropes along the line of molding, one image floods her mind. It was six years ago, he had just turned thirteen. Around dusk the phone rings, rousing Noble from a slumber. A police lieutenant from the Avenue B Station, his voice seems to surge through the phone. Her hands drop the receiver, as two words reply in her mind: not again, not again. "Is this Mrs. McDaniel? We have a Dambalah Rogers in our custody". Her heart begins its banging, "attempted rape and aggravated assault". She drops the receiver again. "He has spoken with an attorney." I better put some clothes on. "You better come on down here ma'am. . . ." Attempted rape. In custody. Avenue B Station. After contacting a bailbondsman, Miss Settle drives her over to the station. Dambalah is standing flush at the bars of his cell. His eyes cast out at whoever approached. His fists clenching the bars: I will not look at him. Lt. M. asks did she know X? did she see Y? Then another officer. Then a young Puerto Rican lawyer. Another grandmother whose grandson beat a girl nearly to death. Somebody else, somebody else, until finally, Noble's knees buckle her right onto the concrete floor. What she remembers next: She is standing right before this door, yelling at Dambalah, telling him she has had enough, she is putting him out. "You gotta get outta here boy, I can't take this no more. I'm seventy-one years old! You drove your whole family away and your grandfather to an early grave, and you still don't let up. Now you gonna get outta here!" This reply: "I ain't going nowhere," before he leaps at her, slamming her back into the wall behind her. She hears something snap, my hip? my leg? my arm? what? Blackness, then

Miss Settle is standing over her: "Ms. Noble, are you okay? What happened? are you awright?" Noble sits up, while her shoulders and right hip afire with pain. "I'm fine, thank you Mary Ann, thank you very much." Verifying that nothing is broken, her only considerations becoming the condition of Dambalah: "Where is he? Is he hurt? How long was I out?" Until Miss Settle quiets her down with: "He's fine, don't worry about him, ma'am. He came and got me right after you fell . . . Are you sure you are okay?" Noble says nothing, complicitly nodding her affirmation.

The fingertips of her left hand are trembling as she raises them to rap on the door. He's gone have to come out sooner or later. Her hand wavers back and forth, but she cannot bring it to the surface of the stripped wood. She cannot bring herself to knock, she cannot, but then she knocks, knocks, bangs. She hears herself yelling, "Dambalah! Dambalah! Dambalah come outta there. Come out! come out Dambalah! I can't have people shooting into my house. Dambalah baby why does it have to be like this Dambalah!" No answer. Silence, so she knocks again, repeatedly, knocks yelling out his name: "Dambalah! Dambalah! Dambalah!" No answer. Another knock. Her heart is firing away now. She feels a terrible pain come over her upper body. She brings the shotgun to her chest: "Dambalah! Please!" Her hand darts into the right pocket of her cardigan sweater, it fishes around for the huge key ring. It brandishes the key before her face. Sliding the key ring around her wrist, she cocks the shotgun, aims it at the door: "Dambalah baby answer Mama Noble, *Dambalah!*" Once more as she knocks she yells out: "Dambalah baby this time I got to face you!" She turns the key. She turns the knob: She swings the door open. She feels her knees buckling. Her heart is exploding. The cocked gun points into the darkness. Before her hand hits the light switch, she can already see—those blazing eyes, those sunken cheeks, that wild hair, those balled fists–lunging toward her. My God! But the room is empty. Empty. The mattress shows no depression. The air holds no smell. No shoes or socks or underwear lie strewn across the floor. Dambalah. The butt of the shotgun still nestled under her armpit, Noble opens the closet on the left wall of the room. Empty. Dambalah's duffel bag, his shirts, his shoes, everything, gone. She hurries over to the bureau. Every drawer is empty. Her eyes swallow the room. Is he gone? Is he really gone? The makeshift desk. She sees something on the desk. Hunching over it, she reads from a strip of torn newsprint: 1/22, Logan 8:15, call SM—she can barely read the scrawl— meet S at . . . Her eyes roll off this onto a carefully folded piece of notebook paper. Setting the shotgun down, Noble checks behind her. She is alone. Slowly she unfolds the page. She can no longer feel her heart beating, nor her chest rising. She is not sure if her eyes can focus on the black, block letters covering the page:

mama-had to go
whenevr you talk to my momma
tell her I love her,
yr dambalah.

"Oh my God," Noble cries out, swaying back and forth; the sheet of paper rattling in her hands. Her vision swirls from one point in the room to another. Oh my God, oh my God, he's gone, he's gone, he's gone. Oh my God, just like his mother he up and left me. Oh my God Lord Jesus what am I supposed to do? Lord Jesus he's gone! Her hands still clutching fast to the letter, she feels her knees starting to give way. He's gone! She reaches out to the desk, grabs ahold of its edge. He's gone! She snatches up the piece of newsprint, stuffing it in the right pocket of her cardigan. He's gone. She refolds the letter carefully, placing it gingerly on top of the scrap of newsprint. Turning, she examines the room once more, for something, for what? examining, scouring, until she finally turns off the light, pulling the door closed behind her. Dambalah. One long, last breath, before she turns the key until she hears the lock click. Backing away from the door, her left hand searches for the molding outside. He's gone. She paces herself down the hall. Her right hand holding tightly that folded note. When she reaches the end of the hallway, she turns around, to nothing but a deserted passageway full of dim light and her own heavy smell. A throbbing begins in her breasts. Her stomach floods with pain. Her hand crumples the letter in her pocket. *He's gone.* Dambalah.▲

Mark Mills was born in Kingston, Jamaica. He attended Tilden High School in East Flatbush, Brooklyn, and Cornell University. His poetry and reviews have appeared in *Obsidian II* and *The Village Voice* respectively. He is currently completing his first novel, *Ran*. Mark Mills lives in New York City.▲

I AND I

by MARK MILLS

Now I'm in this van . . .

DON'T!

All I want is my money: the cash Shakim owes me. Loaned him a C over the summer cuz we'z boys back in the day—or else I wouldn't a loaned him shit. He's working the slopes for Jus, using too. But he hooked me last semester when I was short for books, so I said, "Okay, Shak, I'll put you D." But now financial aid said the loan I was supposed to get—I ain't getting. Counselor said shit's more "stringent." So now I need *all* my money.

"Don't worry 'bout it, homeboy. Meet me up on the boulevard at 4 o'clock CCNY is on me . . ."

5 o'clock came and the boy wasn't nowhere near Adam Clayton Powell! More like Malcolm X.

DON'T NOBODY!

So I cut through a couple lots, jet into the burnt out building, climb the rickety stairs, and knock on 2B's sheet metal door.
    "Yo Shakim, it's me!"
    The door opens. Him and his boys scaling serious snow on the triple beam. House beats pumping. One light bulb dangling from the chipped ceiling. Everybody talking 'bout "getting paid in full, paid in full, paid in full." He's trying to get me to chill, but I'm not wit it: "Yo, Shak, just hook me so I can break."

DON'T—DON'T NOBODY MOVE!

German Sheppards on our ass. Shotguns pumped. 45's aimed. No time to think twice. Cuffs crunch, lock, rip into skin. A tear streams down my face, mixing with the dirt and gravel I'm trying to spit out the side of my mouth. The Beast's forearm on my neck, flashlight in my eye. My wallet opened, pressed against my face.
    "You Owen Chandler?"
    "Yeah!"
    "You're going to have a lot of time to study now."

    Now I'm in this van . . .
    No light. No ventilation. Can't hardly breathe from the smell of sweat and anger. Babylon production in full effect, a Neo-Middle Passage

constructed by the Beast. Rough riding to Brooklyn, borough of kings, 20 of us—shackled, arms, legs, chain-gang style. Trying to remember how to breathe, how to jail house box, how to roll a winning combo for celo—is it 4-5-6? Damn! I Need all my knowledge from the university of the streets. *"I'm sorry, there's less money this year. Don't you have family or relatives you can borrow the money from? . . . Guidelines are more stringent, this year. . .*

Chill, I and I . . . seen all a that: False concern manifesting existentially. Unviable options from casa blanca colonizers. *Ronnie, The Sequel,* cold rockin' the Establishment's collegiate version of the IRS. Voodoo Poppy called it. Education, of the oppressed, take one, take two, take ad infinitum. For real this time . . . again. Bet—I and I, speak, seen, to me, all a that—word.

Alchemizing foundations of tinsel and bad luck like Drew and transfusions. EZ, my knowledge, myself . . . I and I . . . through the eye of the needle . . . can still see Medina, whole. Cuz this is Maasai from the Nile . . . just in wrong place, wrong time, not destiny . . .

I and I . . . seen all a that.▲

Jess Mowry was born in Mississippi in 1960 and raised in Oakland, where he was educated through the eighth grade. In 1988 he bought a used typewriter for ten dollars and started writing. His first book of stories, *Rats in the Trees*, won the PEN Oakland/Josephine Miles Award in 1990. Jess' most recent work is the novel *Way Past Cool,* which has been critically acclaimed. He lives in Oakland.▲

ANIMAL RIGHTS. . .

by JESS MOWRY

. . . organizers in the Bay Area joined today in voicing support of an activist group claiming responsibility for vandalizing property in Santa Cruz County. The office and adjoining structure of a small business was ransacked, files destroyed, and a blood-like substance was splashed over wall and floors. According to a spokesperson for the activists, animals, primarily white rabbits, rats and mice, were being raised on the premises for the purpose of laboratory experimentation. Cages were destroyed and all animals removed. The spokesperson refused to disclose where the animals were taken, saying only, 'to a place of refuge and safety.' The spokesperson declined further comment, adding only that, 'animals have no one to speak up for them and their welfare should be the concern of every caring human being.' Authorities are still investigating. In local news, last night's drive-by shooting of an East Oakland youth. . .

The boy stared at the TV screen, not hearing much more than the soothing cadence of the white lady's voice, or seeing anything but shifting colors. Dimly, he remembered his mom telling him something . . . a long time ago . . . about *in one ear and out the other.* That was cool. Nothing stayed inside long enough to hurt.

The boy sat small, deep in the big old couch. It was covered in worn-out red velvet, but enough of the nap remained to feel soft on his body. There were no sharp angles to hurt him. He wore only jeans; faded 501s that were a little too small so three of the buttons were open. They too were soft against his skin. The open buttons kept them from pinching. That was cool. Nothing hurt, and they were probably better than what he'd been wearing before . . .

Before what?

In one ear and out the other.

The TV voices droned on and the pretty colors shifted. If the boy thought hard enough he might remember that this was the early morning news. Soon there would be cartoons. He didn't know how long he'd been watching the screen; all night, weeks . . . or years. It didn't matter. He drifted at peace in softness and warmth. If he concentrated he might have remembered more, but nothing hurt so there was no reason to remember.

The boy was maybe ten, his skin like ebony velvet, with eyes that looked large and lost in a small peaceful face, long-lashed and gentle obsidian. His body was just beginning to take on the puppy-look of major growing. He was thin. Small, tight muscles had started to define chest and arms, but now seemed slack and fading as if no longer needed. His hair was bushy and wild, but clean, and scented with lice shampoo. Sometimes he was given a bath. Since when, he couldn't remember, but it didn't matter. Here he was, and nothing hurt.

There were cartoons. "The Teenage Mutant Ninja Turtles." Vaguely he recalled it being a cool show that he liked. But now he couldn't remember their names.

The man's voice came from over his shoulder. "Boy! You got to go?"

The boy considered the words. What did they mean? He half turned his head toward the voice, but then forgot why. It didn't seem important.

"Shit!" said the voice. Then, "Irene! Get his ass to the bathroom fore he go and mess himself again!"

The boy didn't like the voice when it sounded that way. Maybe it reminded him of something? The woman came . . . Irene . . . and took his hand. It was a surprise to discover he could stand . . . that his legs held him up even though he walked on clouds. It was a surprise to find he *could* walk; to see his very own bare feet way down on carpet and then cross faded green linoleum one step at a time. Green like grass. He hadn't walked on much grass in his life. Even the linoleum felt soft. Linoleum grass. A new idea. The woman . . . Irene . . . set him on the toilet. He wondered if that should piss him off. After all, he wasn't a goddamn baby, and boys stood on their own two feet to piss. But that didn't seem to matter to the woman. Maybe she just wanted to be safe? He supposed he should do something, but seemed to have forgotten what it was. He was aware of the woman's hands, soft and warm on his bare shoulders, holding him. Her voice was carelessly gentle. "C'mon, boy, do somethin for mama fore you go noddin again."

The boy had a name, but couldn't remember it. The woman . . . Irene, wasn't really his mother. Maybe he did do something in the toilet because he found he was standing on his own special feet once more, and the woman was buttoning his jeans. All but the top three. She led him back to the couch. There were more cartoons, but he wasn't sure what they were about. The old velvet was soft, but it seemed important to remember his name. Why?

The man's voice: "For chrissake, feed him, Irene! Saturday busy as hell . . . be goddamn 'barrasin he die on us!" Laughter.

No, Irene wasn't really his mother. But mostly she was kinder than his mother had been. Even the man was kind in his way, though not as gentle-voiced anymore as when he'd picked the boy up in his big new car and brought him here. Wherever *here* was. It didn't matter. Here was a lot better than *there*. Here was warm and soft and nothing hurt.

Except . . .

The boy wasn't sure. Not yet. But he almost remembered.

A spoonful of color appeared under his small snub nose. Lucky Charms. Marshmallow shapes. Pretty. A spoonful of sweetness fed to him. He concentrated on not choking. Milk dribbled down his chin and chest. The woman clucked her tongue gently, the way his mother had done long ago. A soft cloth cleaned him up. Good as new. When had his mother been so kind? A long time before he'd come home from school to find the apartment empty? He was starting to remember. The Lucky Charms were sweet and crunchy, and the marshmallows melted to warm syrupy goo in his mouth. The woman was gentle as she fed him, waiting until he remembered to swallow, sometimes reminding him to. Did love him? Most times she was kind . . . except when he messed himself like a goddamn baby. Or choked. Or forgot what to do on the toilet. Then she would shake him. Sometimes she'd shake him for no reason he could figure, but she never hit him. Even the man was kind in his way . . . he didn't want him to die.

The cartoons were almost making sense now. If he blinked his eyes and thought mega-hard he could remember things . . . fog drifting through the night streets, following him. Streetlamps haloed, cold, wet, and lonely. He shivered. It hurt to remember.

A knock on the door. Men-voices, mostly the man. He had a name . . . a street name . . . but the boy couldn't remember it. Yet. Maybe if he could remember his own it would help? If he concentrated with all his might he could just understand the men's words . . .

"I tellin ya, Jack, be prime product I got here."

"Yeah? And how I know that, man? Could be death in a sandwich. Don't know you from nobody. Your price be the only thing I *know* prime, for a fact!"

The boy looked down at his arm. Sometimes it hurt. Things weren't supposed to hurt. It said on TV that it shouldn't hurt to be a kid. The man-voices, rising and falling, reminded him of that.

"Shit, man! You got to take nuthin on faith! Not from me. Come along here and check this out. Right from the bag, see? You watchin?"

The boy stirred. The TV screen blurred. His arm hurt again and he began to remember. His name! Almost, he had it!

Man-shapes standing over him. Tenseness in the air. Smells of suspicion. Men-voices again. "Yo! Check this out. My own son here! Boy I love. Word up!"

The pain of the needle, sharp in his arm. Man-laughter. "Yo! He look like he dyin to you, man? Hell, watch him long's you like."

More laughter. The voices fading . . . fading like the pain until nothing hurt anymore. All was softness and warmth, and sometimes even a gentle touch.

So why, the boy wondered, was he crying?▲

Lisa Teasley A native of Los Angeles, Lisa Teasley's fiction and poetry have been published in *Rampike, Between C & D, Event, Catalyst, L.A. Weekly, The New Renaissance, Artline, Rohwedder, Amelia* and *Westwind*. She is awaiting publication in the *Great River Review*. Teasley is also a contributing editor for the Beyond Baroque Literary Foundation magazine, *Forehead*. Her poems which appear in the book: *Women For All Seasons*, were described by one reviewer as having "a passionate sensuality (indeed a passion and an anger that probe and linger, that tear apart, and threaten to break out of the fairly rote structure). . ."

Teasley won the May Merrill Miller Award in 1984 for fiction, the 1988 Los Angeles Chapter, National Society of Arts & Letters Short Story Award, and the 1992 Amaranth Review Award for Short Fiction. She graduated from UCLA with a degree in English, specializing in creative writing. Teasley is currently an artist-in-residence at the Manhattan Beach Public Arts Program, funded by the California Arts Council, where she teaches poetry and short fiction.

A painter as well, Teasley exhibits extensively throughout California areas. Her paintings were featured in the movie *Deep Cover.*▲

THE LIVE BURIAL OF BERYL FUQUA

by LISA TEASLEY

"Every form corrrectly seen is beautiful."
—GOETHE

That was when we found her dancing with the dead birds. She had them laid out in a circle 'round her, skirt hiked up on her thighs, eyes red as the bulb on a thermometer. She didn't stop just 'cause we were there, don't think she even saw us. It was as if she were an apparition, her face hopeful and calm as a monk's.

Beryl's life had been bizarre to say the least; too much had gone down hard for her twenty-one years. The only control she had was when she put the curse down with her mother's corpse, just before they shoveled her in. People found it hard to believe that she could think about a lover when they were burying her mother and her twin. But the thing is, they never stopped or bothered to think about why. We used to hang with her and Cheryl, before Cheryl died. The two of them would dress in wild colors, matching to a T. We would match each other, and people would gawk at the foursome we made, fascinated to see two sets of twins.

But Beryl wasn't no witch, 'though she used to play this game with Cheryl. We mean, Beryl's curse just worked on old Tommy T. 'cause it's a Panamanian superstition. When a written curse goes down with a corpse at the burial, the curse is gonna work. And old Tommy T. had played Beryl for a fool, real good. We just didn't think she might still be thinking about that so close to the horrible incident that killed her mother and her twin. But we're getting ahead of ourselves. Then again, maybe there's no order to this.

So back to the game with Cheryl. Beryl had this game called Sea Witch. We think it had something to do with her losing her cherry in the ocean. On the jungle hot days when there was no way we were gonna sit up in a classroom, we'd just ditch and head for the beach near the Canal Zone. Beryl had always tended to be a bit faster than Cheryl, and so after she met old Tommy T. we were all sure it would be just a matter of when, and not whether. Tommy T. came sniffing 'round with his tongue hanging out, and Beryl decided he was fine. He was ugly to us: his head was square and flat on top, his eyes glassy, his body way too long. But he was older, and Beryl liked the possibilities of a graying man, so she let herself be sniffed up and down. And he kept saying all these trite things like, the blacker the berry the sweeter the juice. And Beryl being so black, blacker than Cheryl, and people calling Cheryl the prettier for that reason, we thought that Beryl just fell for it. She jumped in the ocean with old Tommy T. in broad, hard daylight. The sun so hot our skin ached and itched. We couldn't see them so good As far as they went out, we didn't even understand how he kept himself standing with the waves and her legs wrapped 'round him. When they came out of the water, his tongue wasn't hanging out. His mouth closed like he was trying to keep all the juices in; and Beryl, who had gone in so fast and sure, came out looking like she didn't know her own name.

So Beryl had decided she was in love after her memory came back. She would meet old Tommy T. every afternoon for at least two months. School wasn't even an issue. Cheryl stayed with us, looking every bit as abandoned as she was. And then when old Tommy T. dumped Beryl for this fat 'ho down in the Spanish part of town, Cheryl was back to herself, and Beryl was back with her twin, only looking haunted.

That was all when Beryl was fifteen. When she and Cheryl turned sixteen, their Mama wanted to take them to the dressmakers for their first black dress. Beryl had this thing about wanting a black satin dress, and of course their Mama would never go for that idea, it being so fast, and so grown a thing to do. But the twins were sixteen, and their Mama finally gave into the idea of them coming out at that age. Now *our* Mama never saw the logic in that, and she thinks that's where everything went wrong for the Fuqua family. She said that twins are a gift from God, an example of man in His image and likeness, set down to show people how much the same we are in His eyes. So she couldn't take to flying in God's face by having her twins come out at sixteen in black, as if twins were just an example of how all women could be the same—whores. So she'd keep us matching in innocent dresses, and we've never dressed any differently, since we had Beryl and Cheryl to do it for us.

On the way to the dressmaker's, Cheryl and her Mama were distracted by the commotion near the factory–bunch of workers striking, and the American police there by the hoards. We don't know the exact story 'cause we weren't there, but we heard that somehow Cheryl and Beryl's mama got struck on the head by the police, and that's when Cheryl cracked her control and tried to jump the pig who did it; biting at his neck until he beat her to a pulp. This is only what we heard. In fact, it could all be twisted. 'Cause if you bring up that whole mess now about the Fuquas, people act like they have a memory loss.

Don't ask why Beryl didn't go to the dressmaker's. It was her idea to begin with. She probably just plum didn't want to go. It doesn't make sense at all. But we were talking about the Sea Witch game, and then we got off track realizing how this could all be misinterpreted. Beryl was never a witch, never possessed, and never evil. She was just fast, and too imaginative for her own good. That's all.

When they found Beryl at nineteen with the gun in her hand, she was simply in shock. Tommy T. was already a long gone memory, so she had fallen in love again with Sweet Jeremy. The curse had put Tommy T. in a wheelchair—he seemed to have gotten polio from out of nowhere—still we know it was Beryl. No one talked about old Tommy T.'s dilapidation into death, but it was pretty common knowledge that it was Beryl's curse that did it. Back to Sweet Jeremy.

Jeremy actually asked Beryl to marry him. He had a steady job, working the boats at the Canal. But then Jeremy one day comes in to announce that he had joined the service. Beryl was sitting up in his house, playing with the gold that Jeremy melted into jewelry just for her. We don't know how much gold he had, we just know that Beryl had all these things with her name and Jeremy's 'round her neck, or on her wrist in gold. And she was sitting up in his house, where he also lived with his ancient mother, playing with the gold when he announced he was going to service. We don't exactly know, but we heard that Beryl took it well at first. But Beryl had this thing about blood that sickened her, gave her nightmares, and the war was going on at that time. So we guess she vividly imagined Sweet Jeremy going off to war, and she waiting home for the bloody corpse to come back. She must have shot him in the foot to keep him home. They made up all that stuff about Jeremy having cheated on her, and that being the reason for her shooting him. But we know for a fact that Jeremy was just too sweet. That's why we thought it such a shame they had to cut off his foot. Beryl couldn't live with him and her guilt after that, so they didn't even get married. They just drifted apart. That was the true tragedy of Beryl's life.

But we keep getting sidetracked from the Sea Witch game. The one that people had seen and decided it supported their theory that Beryl was an evil spirit, a witch, whatever they liked to call it. But she wasn't. She just liked the ocean at night, and she tried to drag Cheryl into it 'cause she wanted to share everything with her. I think she wanted Cheryl to understand why she was so moved by the experience with old Tommy T. in the ocean. We think she likened sex somehow to being in the ocean. Beryl would take the seaweed and wrap it 'round Cheryl's body. Usually Cheryl was naked, but sometimes she had her panties on. And Beryl would talk to Cheryl, whisper to her in this sweet lull of a voice, luring Cheryl into the ocean as Beryl followed close behind. Every time they would go just a bit farther out, and when it was too far and they'd had their dance of dare with the undertow, Beryl would lift Cheryl's body as they floated, drifted, or were thrown back to shore. Cheryl would usually be somewhat unconscious with the trance. We don't know what Beryl whispered to her, but we know it would get louder as they went out farther into the ocean, then softer again as they came back in. With that and the sound of the waves, Cheryl would be spellbound, and her body, her dark, brown body with the snaked, slimy ropes of seaweed, her lips real raw from biting down on them, made her look like some under-earth princess, violated in some way that made her desirable 'cause of it. We know that the more Beryl dragged Cheryl into the ocean, the more men there were buzzing 'round her wherever they went. Beryl called Cheryl the Sea Witch, after the game had become a regular thing. Cheryl would passively answer to it everyday until her death.

So when we found Beryl dancing with the dead birds that day, it wasn't any kind of surprise. We stood there watching for a long time, 'cause she was captivating in her brilliant red skirts, a tight, torn black satin top just enough to cover long, lovely titties. We don't know if she killed the birds on the beach that night, and we really doubt that she did 'cause she is not evil. We told them that when they came to take her away. Of course they wouldn't listen to a couple of sad-faced twins. We never had an impact on anyone, besides some momentary fascination they might have had with a double vision. But that's nothing like the lifelong fascination we had with Beryl, who was never the daring half of a twin. She was whole, and she was *beautiful.*▲

Artress Bethany White was born in Boston, MA and rooted in FL. She is a graduate of the University of Massachusetts, Amherst where she received her Bachelor of Arts degree. Her work has appeared in the literary journal *Callaloo*. Other forthcoming work will appear in *Muleteeth*, a journal being published by the Dark Room Writers Collective based in Boston, MA, of which she is a member. She is currently living in New York, where she teaches English at Long Island University, Brooklyn.▲

MOONSHINER, GIFTHORSE AND GHOST F.A. CHANCE

by ARTRESS BETHANY WHITE

Moonshiner uses the familiar gesture of running his hand across his forehead whenever put in a position to contemplate what his life could have been. The first time he was seen doing this was during his waning boyhood days.

Moonshiner had come to understand that, regardless of bygone manhood ritual, the African Four-Fathers would never think of abandoning him. Their blood-rushing voices leapt through his body, waking him from sweat drenched sleep, shaking his bed with their message-laden drumbeats. Guiding him with multiple foot-thumping voices retelling stories that left him limp with terror.

Somehow he came to the conclusion that the single rule of this age-old game was inscribed on the underside of his belly. He undressed in the dark to avoid it, but he could still feel it there pressing to emerge.

Finding himself faced with only two choices of salvation, he turned to his mother and father. His father appeared to handle internal commotion well. Cloaked in yards if Italian cloth and woodland scent. Moonshiner would stand poised around the corner of a room, watching and waiting for an appropriate opening. But he never witnessed any of his fathers muscle contortions hinting at communion with the Four-Fathers. Not even a flicker to reflect his own private hell. His father appeared so controlled in fact that sometimes it was as if he wasn't even there.

Moonshiner next approached his mother, believing she may have assisted his father in some supernatural, feminine way. He initiated a careful camaraderie by gently tapping her on the backside with his open palm as he had seen his father do. In a heartbeat he found himself laid out, contemplating the innermost complexities of the kitchen's linoleum floor.

Moonshiner quickly decided he would have to wait for salvation to come to him. Just as he was readying himself to let down his guard and try to make sense of the Four-Fathers rousing beat, an apparition appeared, temptingly willow-bending toward him. Ivory cool limbs open to embrace.

Not stopping to question the Four-Fathers, with whom he had yet to build up a rapport, on their opinion of this pale and understanding newcomer, he snatched at the saving hand.

Almost instantly he felt a new sense of control. He was buoyed into manhood, unfettered by blood-rushing drumbeats. Nestling his head against the proffered knee, he began to take on the ideals of this wondrous stepfather. Discovering new rules to guide him that could fit on pages, and were easy to decipher. He learned to speak a rhythmless language, clean and flat with no emotional valleys to get lost in.

Softly his mother, father, brothers and sisters fell away from him along with his dark, heavy old skin. Extra weight removed, he glided freely heavenward. The higher he flew, the less he thought of looking down. He had tried once, all rites of passage demanding a last look back at what was left behind. His head, however, had begun to reel, his body twisting mid-air seeking to plummet him, head-first, into self-awareness. He screamed, fighting the opening of his mind, and clawing at his eyes forced them heavenward again.

After that Moonshiner grew to respect his adoption. To drink thirstily of the pristine bored-room. Practicing the sympathetic nod. Sitting comfortably high and away from the hog, watching it rut from atop his altar rock. He became adept at following his stepfather's rulebook so as not to rock his fragile perch.

Moonshiner feels strong now. Not of character or stature. These terms are meaningless in his world. He displays his strength in mental dexterity. A flamboyant tap dance of thought. He wears a standard moonshiner smile. Bending over frequently for maximum wattage. First flashed in the mirror upon waking, then saluting himself smartly, minus the heel tap that might scuff his shoes. Shoes of well stitched, ox-blood red that allow him to glide past any ghostly images he may encounter on his way to join the slim ranks of his fellow moonshiners.

The Four-Fathers call out to Moonshiner but have yet to get a response; their drumbeats losing resonance when filtered through the stepfathers world. Still, they look on, patient smiles resting on their lips, confident of Moonshiners eventual return.

*****

Walking along the street, Gifthorse indulges in one of his favorite scenarios. Passing a shuffling ghost, he drops a few coins into the black-lined, outstretched palm, pausing only long enough to flash a beatific smile into the sunken face.

After dozens of these missions, Gifthorse has suddenly gained new insight into the meaning of his life. Much deliberation has led him to discover how he can truly lend substance to the lives of his ghostly brothers. He would take on the burden of bringing their abandoned culture to complete fruition. Elevate it from primitive ruin with the Gifthorses' knack for rediscovery. Wrapping himself tightly in the ivory mantle of the sainted, he ran home to tell his father that his life was worth something after all.

His father bowed his head solemnly as Gifthorse outlined his strategy. Then raising his eyes heavenward in fond memory, he began to relate how his generation had opened its arms to the fatherless ghosts. Sharing their mysteriously abundant legacy, so that ghosts wouldn't exorcise themselves right out of the picture. Then carefully extracting a few exceptional ghosts to fashion into Moonshiners in the Gifthorse image.

Ironically, at this point in his tale, his father's pale, gesturing hands passed before the dining room walls, where various wood-carved and vividly painted portraits of African Four-Fathers hung in profusion.

Gifthorse swore that he could see their eyes glaring beneath hooded, wooden slits. Their regal warrior faces snarl. After several rapid blinks, however, he decided that he had been mistaken.

He again gave his full attention to his father, who had just been getting to the part about the butter rising off the cream—manifested in the current crop of Moonshiner nobility.

Gifthorse now dedicates himself to vigorous labor. He has taken to the field with widened vision, clear of brow sweat. Traveled back to the continent where the ghosts had last clasped hands with the Four-Fathers in earth-thumping chant. Attempting to enrich his life with stropping song and underbelly rhythms, emoted in a prayerful tongue. He has learned to speak the language of the Four-Fathers with precise, grammatical intonation. His Wolof is particularly sound.

On occasion, he becomes so enraptured with newfound joy that he starts to speak to passing ghosts in their long-lost tongue. Then, true to his namesake, he snaps his lips shut before they can peer into his sacrilegious mouth.

Gifthorse regularly sits in a brightly lit hall along with eight or nine others. Each has a drum held uneasily between their knees. Poker faces on fire, they strain, blue veins and eyes popping, to beat their way into the hearts of the Four-Fathers. Leading the, as usual, well-intentioned troops is icy-eyed Gifthorse, trying to substitute technique and fervor for rhythm.

The Four-Fathers watch Gifthorse, quietly shaking their heads humph, humph, humph. Refusing to touch their drums in answer to his accentless beats.

*****

Ghost F.A. Chance has been slapped down more times than he can remember. His back is bent, stomach swollen, legs crippled. They always seemed to catch him before he could open his eyes.

Ghost had always run a fast race, despite his physical hardship. Between striving to reach Moonshiner and cursing Gifthorse, eating all their leavings and still coming up empty. Every time his fellows tried with twenty hands to support his chin, some new paralysis of the mind would befall him.

It appeared that he had taken all the right precautions. He had learned the rules, then, pushing forward made it to within spitting distance of the altar rock gate. At which point a whole new rulebook for entrance would fall down past him, and he would go off scurrying again.

Increasingly disillusioned, he walked aimlessly, trying to get a grip on his amorphous self. On one of his journeys, carefully spitting before taking a step, ensuring that he would adhere to the cement, he saw Moonshiner hurrying toward him. Excitement bubbled up inside him. It was rare that such nobility came within his range.

Caught up in his elation, Ghost began calling to his long-lost brother, hoping to get some answers to a few things that had been on his mind. He began uttering a language, the cadence of which was oddly reminiscent of that spoken by the Four-Fathers.

Startled, Moonshiner looked up at him, familiar terror ringing in his eyes. Recoiling, he scuttled away, looking over his shoulder and passing his hand anxiously across his forehead. Ghost watched Moonshiner until he finally stopped two corners away for a shoeshine.

Returning dejectedly to his usual thinking place, Ghost sat waiting for Gifthorse to make his ritualistic pass. Gifthorse appeared, seeming to levitate an inch above the sidewalk, as saints will. He stopped in front of Ghost, never failing to understand his suffering, and dropped a coin into his outstretched palm, pausing only long enough to grace him with a beatific smile.

Soon after, Ghost had a sudden revelation. Any spectators would have quickly looked away from the somewhat sinister grin that split his face. Both Moonshiner and Gifthorse had seemed very preoccupied. Could it be that Ghost's own anonymity was perhaps an asset?

Ghost F.A. Chance has since taken up carpentry. He has managed to accumulate quite a respectable pile of wooden blocks. Things move rather slowly though. Picking up a block, he passes it on to each of his fellows, and everyone examines it until each has a feel for its purpose. Then carefully setting it aside they pick up another.

Ghost doesn't know for sure what they will end up building, but remarkably the process has resulted in each of his fellows acquiring the habit of speaking one at a time. That is, when they speak at all. Most of their attention is focused inward on the echoing rhythms of blood-rushing voices, riding on a steady drumbeat. The Four-Fathers, avid gamblers, could never resist aligning themselves with a sure thing.▲